The Traveling and Writing Self

I0643748

The Traveling and Writing Self

Edited by

Marguerite Helmers and Tilar Mazzeo

Cambridge Scholars Publishing

The Traveling and Writing Self, Edited by Marguerite Helmers and Tilar Mazzeo

This book first published 2007. The present binding first published 2008.

Cambridge Scholars Publishing

12 Back Chapman Street, Newcastle upon Tyne, NE6 2XX, UK

British Library Cataloguing in Publication Data
A catalogue record for this book is available from the British Library

Copyright © 2008 by Marguerite Helmers and Tilar Mazzeo and contributors

All rights for this book reserved. No part of this book may be reproduced, stored in a retrieval system, or transmitted, in any form or by any means, electronic, mechanical, photocopying, recording or otherwise, without the prior permission of the copyright owner.

ISBN (10): 1-4438-0043-0, ISBN (13): 978-1-4438-0043-3

TABLE OF CONTENTS

CHAPTER ONE

UNRAVELING THE TRAVELING SELF

MARGUERITE HELMERS & TILAR MAZZEO

Why do people travel? What is the relationship between the experience and the writing of the journey? How much of the traveler's tale is truth, and how much is fiction? These questions lie at the heart of travel scholarship. The vast body of work constituting "travel literature" ranges from the time of Herodotus to the present. Its genres include tales of exploration, ships' logs, private journals and letters, magazine articles, and a sizeable body of fanciful tales produced by those whom Percy Adams called "travel liars." The motives for travel change, the writing styles differ, and the interpretation of the text can vary, but readers sense that, as travelers write about their experiences, they capture more than descriptions of place: they reveal something of their time, place, personality, circumstances, and prejudices.

This collection of essays on travel writing came together after the Fourth Biennial Conference on Travel Writing, held in Milwaukee, Wisconsin in 2004 and hosted by the International Society for Travel Writing. The theme of the conference was "The Voyage Out," an allusion to the work of Virginia Woolf and a literal reference to a significant theme in the writing of travel. For, while much writing about travel has emphasized the arrival at the destination, the voyage itself was filled with interest, adventure, and peril. Travelers always set out from somewhere. That space is usually the familiar "home," to which the anticipated and often exotic "away" of the travels is contrasted. Voyaging outward is attended by a cumulative ideology that shapes the traveler's experience.

The essays in this collection indicate an emerging strain in the study of travel writing from the Romantic era to the present, focusing on the narrative structure of the text and the self-crafted persona of the traveler-protagonist. As its unifying principle, this book examines some of the relationships that can be discerned when travel writing, autobiography, and fiction are placed side by side for study. In this chapter, we highlight some of the ideas that are implicit in this collection: the desire of travelers to discover that which is "new"; the narrative negotiation between an outward self and an inner self; the concept that the writer's self is a fiction; the notion that writers use perceptual templates to understand and describe places; the transitional, liminal experience of passage; the dialogic nature of vision, which holds that the observer is also observed; and the constructed nature of place when it is construed as a storyworld.

A rich discussion of authorial self has been initiated in the field of anthropology. The relationship of the writer's mediating perception to the objects of study has been at the root of questions about ethnography for several decades, giving rise to a subgenre of "auto-ethnography," in which the anthropologist consciously works to bring biases and perceptual difficulties to the forefront and does not seek to occlude his or her own sensibilities behind an authorial, authoritative voice. It is perhaps axiomatic that travel writers and anthropologists infuse their view of the new and the different with their own backgrounds and preoccupations. The discourses used to describe places that are remote from the writer's home and the people who inhabit these news lands; the awareness of an eventual readership (however fictionalized and constructed), composed of like-minded citizens of the homeland; and the inescapable points of view shaped by Western culture have all contributed to a long history of imperial literature. Critics who have written about travel and ethnography—Edward Said, Mary Louise Pratt, Chandra Mohanty, Gillian Rose, among others—have invoked terms such as "imaginative geography" and "imperial eyes" to describe the pervasive Western gaze and point of view that infuses the narratives of travelers. The discourse of travelers from the seventeenth, eighteenth, and nineteenth centuries was based upon differences, oppositions between those who have and have not: urban/rural, Christian/pagan, literate/illiterate, civilized/savage. At the same time, as Mary Louise Pratt notes, there was a certain redundancy to the accounts. The repetitive nature of the encounter with the "savage," for example, crossed centuries. Likewise, the search for differences was often tempered by a comparative rhetoric, in which the unique culture or language was translated in terms of familiar practices, objects, or texts. These important critical investigations remind scholars of the importance of point of view, narratorial construction, and codes of representation used to describe and imagine another culture and another set of experiences.

Voyage of Discovery

The primary works examined in this collection date from the eighteenth century to the present, an extended period in which the concept of the modern "self" was constructed and refined through philosophical and literary debate. The authors in this volume agree that, while the impetus to write the journey varies, perception of place is mediated by social and literary ways of seeing, and no experience is either simply or transparently committed to the page. In fact, much modern travel was driven by the need to discover the unique or "new." European exploration literature by the beginning of the Romantic period was focused primarily on the articulation of a self that was increasingly bound up with the interests of commerce and science. The most unique and compelling voyages of the era described the competition to find the source of the Nile and the location of Timbuktu. Even Mary Wollstonecraft's intensely personal and reflective account of her travels in Scandinavia at the turn of the century—letters that contemporaries described as having the power to make men fall in love with the author—were written in the context of a business mission undertaken during war time. In her study *Solitary Travelers: Nineteenth-Century Women's Travel Narratives and the Scientific Vocation*, Lila Marz Harper analyzes the importance of scientific inquiry in exploration accounts from this period. Various critics have described the search for the new, constructed as part of the rhetoric of colonial expansion and the classification of the exoticized and unfamiliar other, beginning with the seminal work of Edward Said and Mary Louise Pratt and continued in studies such as Inderpal Grewal's *Home and Harem: Nation, Gender, Empire, and the Cultures of Travel.*

As Karen Lawrence has observed, the object of the travel writer—to describe an experience that is unique and that sees the world, known or unknown, in a new way—is complicated by an inevitable sense of belatedness. By the beginning of the eighteenth century, Lawrence argues, we see an "almost desperate attempt in…travel writing to make it new, to find a new angle from which to cast a travel book [that] recognizes that it was getting harder and harder to be first" (24). By the turn of the nineteenth century, Lord Byron lamented that there was little point in his describing Constantinople because "you have read fifty descriptions by sundry travelers" (1: 274), and the route of the Grand Tourist was broadly familiar to British readers and writers by at least the middle of the preceding century. By the end of the nineteenth century, very few regions of the world remained unexplored, but the anxiety persisted.[1] Despite this reality, however, the search for the new and the novel remained the ideal of travel writers and their publishers, who continued to believe that readers would be attracted to accounts that offered, if not new locales, at least new insights and new ways of experiencing the familiar.

In early American travel writing, this effort to describe both exploration and national identity in ways that were new and distinct from the European Old World can be seen in the works of Henry David Thoreau, whose descriptions of the Maine woods or Walden Pond set out to re-imagine the colonial landscape of early America in ways that reflected the putative novelty and "exceptionalism" of the American national character in the first half-century of the republic. If Thoreau's work testifies to how important this impulse toward the new is in the travel writing, so too do those more familiar travel texts that described the western frontiers of the North-American continent in the nineteenth century. The American idea of the West represents a reiteration of the European effort to describe and to circumscribe imaginatively the New World, and it functions in these works as a *terra incognita* that offers the possibility of exotic indigenous peoples, strange flora and fauna, unimagined commercial potential and natural resources, and the opportunity to write the self in the process of describing what has not been thought before. With the frontier, the effort for the imperialist traveler is relatively uncomplicated. Thoreau's travel texts suggest that this same desire persists in travel writing long after the scenes being described cease to be unfamiliar. Tourists visiting Walden Pond in the present will quickly discover that there is nothing mysterious or isolated about the place. It was not so very different in Thoreau's time. Walden Pond, like the rivers and towns of New England that Thoreau described in his other travel works, were not the empty spaces of the frontier, willing and waiting to receive the inscription of the colonial gaze or the nationalized settler. Yet, Thoreau's impulse as a travel writer was to see the familiar in new ways and as part of new networks of relationships (to philosophy, to nationalism, to spirituality) that made it seem new again. Casey Blanton argues, thinking of Thoreau particularly, that "travel became a metaphor for the way he wanted to live. In this way, perhaps paradoxically but in a peculiarly American fashion, staying at home became a form of travel" (18).

The fashion is not, of course, peculiarly American at all. A generation before Thoreau, Romantic poets such as Robert Southey, Samuel Taylor Coleridge, and William Wordsworth turned their domestic lives in rural England into forms of travel. Homes such as Dove Cottage in Grasmere remain the tourist attractions that, in some respects, they always were intended to be, and travelers continue to descend upon the Lake District in order to see the same sites that Wordsworth described in his *Guide to the English Lakes* (1810). However, the impulse to make the familiar unfamiliar and to describe the unfamiliar as marvelous is one of the central narrative features of travel writing as a trans-historical genre.

Perhaps contemporary travel accounts turn to extreme sports and wilderness survival stories in part precisely because so few landscapes remain to be visited or described for the first time. Tourists, professionally outfitted in gear named after places that were once among the world's most inaccessible (Patagonia, The North Face), are now regularly to be found at Everest base camp, in the backwoods of Alaska, and even at the North Face of the Eiger. The only novelty these experiences can produce is the novelty of catastrophe—instances where everything goes wrong and the traveler is again traversing territory that is *terra incognita.*

The novelty of catastrophe undoubtedly accounts for the transformation of Ground Zero into one of New York City's most popular tourist attractions in the years following the events of September 11, 2001. A recent news report announces how "Travel guides, including *Frommer's* and *Fodor's*, list Ground Zero among the places to see during a Manhattan visit" (Spadora A101). While relatives of those killed at the site find it "a ghoulish form of tourism" ("Outrage at Ground Zero"), tourism to the Lower Manhattan site has numbered in the millions and may even reach nine million visitors once the redevelopment efforts are completed ("Ground Zero Renewal"). Like Thoreau's reinvention of Walden, Americans in the post 9-11 era have come—and have come *en masse*—to see the familiar urban façade of New York City in new ways. The transformation of tragedy into an object of tourism did not begin with Ground Zero, of course. As Chris Rojek argues, these "Black Spots constitute a significant tourist attraction" (62) at sites ranging from "the Auschwitz death camp, the killing fields of Cambodia [to] Kurt Cobain's suicide site in Seattle" (62). Rojek's thesis is that these places of tragedy—what he calls Black Spots—attract tourists precisely because of their power to startle us with the possibility of the disintegration of the familiar. What is new and unexpected seems real: "Crashes, natural disasters, assassinations, and bombings [...] vividly express the collapse of routine and the triumph of the unexpected or the unpredictable" (65). Just as Thoreau's transformation of home into a site of travel was not peculiarly American, the production of this reality effect through catastrophe is also not peculiarly postmodern. Nineteenth-century travelers toured Pompeii and witnessed Italian villages more recently devastated by eruption and earthquakes as part of their tourist itineraries for motivations that seem remarkably similar.

Recently analyzing the construction of Ground Zero as an object of the tourist gaze, Debbie Lisle suggests how powerfully the allure of the new or of the renewed operates both in the articulation of national identity and in the production of tourist desire. The site, Lisle argues, "reproduced [for visitors] powerful feelings of belonging, community and solidarity" (4) and became "a significant cultural site in the reproduction, dissemination and confirmation of a *renewed* American identity [...] this was the primary location for restoring a strong 'America' after the shock of 11 September" (6, emphasis Lisle). The inclination, of course, is to read the transformation of Ground Zero into a mechanism for the production of national consciousness as a reiteration of themes familiar to scholars of travel writing: it becomes the commodification of culture, functions to reify nationalist values and hegemonic cultural identities, and demonstrates the objectification of the gaze. However, Lisle makes the intriguing argument that tourism does not simply function to replicate and "reproduce prevailing norms, values and attitudes" (5). The experience of catastrophe would not be nearly as compelling if this were the case. Instead, tourism at sites like Ground Zero has the potential not only to make the familiar seem unfamiliar but to provoke patterns of perception and experience that are actually different. As every good travel writer knows, the voyage can be transformative, even if the itinerary has been familiar for decades or even centuries.

Voyages of Self

The authors of the essays in this book share a concern with the ways in which the experience of traveling simultaneously constructs and destabilizes the voyager's sense of "self" and personal identity. As Eric Leed points out in his study *The Mind of the Traveler*, the intermediary and often lengthy "passage" from home to away engages the mental and physical aspects of traveling, in many cases altering the body of the traveler through illness or affecting the mind of the traveler through chance encounters with fellow travelers. Leed reminds us that "travel" is a mental and narrative manifestation of a physical act:

> The mental effects of passage—the development of observational skills, the concentration on forms and relations, the sense of distance between an observing self and a world of objects perceived first in their materiality, their externalities and surfaces, the subjectivity of the observer—are inseparable from the physical conditions of movement through space. (Leed 72)

Often, the dialectical making and unmaking of the self is mirrored in the accounts that these travelers composed and is revealed at moments when conventional plots and perceptions give way to narrative rupture, at moments when narrative voices multiply or collapse. The multiplication or bifurcation of the self is a crucial element of the travel narrative as a genre, just as it is in autobiographical genres at large. This raveling and unraveling of the self is particularly fascinating in those texts that undertake most strenuously to represent the "outward" self as unified, stable, and organic. The efforts these writers make to collapse the distance between the personal self and the speaking author are frequently occasions for innovative experiments in that impossible straining for autobiographical realism.

The tension created by the linguistically constructed nature of both the private self and the authorial self is familiar ground both for poststructuralist thinkers and for those engaged in theories of autobiography. As Roland Barthes reminds us, there can be no writing of the self that coincides with the fragmentary and transitory passage of lived experience: "the one *who speaks* (in the narrative) is not the one *who writes* (in real life) and the one *who writes* is not the one *who is*" (261). Citing the work of Claude Bremond, Paul Ricouer proposes that self-identity depends on "the attribution of some [...] predicate-process to a subject-person" (Bremond qtd. in Ricouer 144). It depends, in other words, on ascribing characteristics of action (the predicate) to the actor (the subject-person). The self is constructed as a means of making sense of events that would otherwise remain incoherent. This interconnection between being and time that Ricoeur proposes enables readers of travel writing and ethnography to envision different aspects of the self. As Andrea Stöckl describes this belatedness of the self:

> The self we write about is turned into "an Other" when we progress in time. Thus, who we think we are when we write a text is already another self. We can thus know and write about our selves from a limited perspective [...] If we create ourselves as an ego in the text, we should be aware that it is not always our selves we are talking about. (Stöckl n.p.)

While important generic differences exist between travel writing and autobiography—perhaps most importantly that the autobiographer writes to an audience that is often first the self and only secondarily other, while the travel writer, though employing the "I," typically writes for a public audience—autobiographical theory stresses that all representation of the self, like memory itself, is selective, self-censoring, and constructed, an effort to impose the fiction of narrative unity and coherence on our lives and on the lives of others. Thus, any account purporting to offer a complete truth about an "elsewhere" must be treated as the product of a traveling, writing "self," one with a constructed narrative point-of-view.[2]

This has particular implications for how we understand the autobiographical and self-replicating strategies of narrative, including travel narrative, employed by writers located for reasons of race, class, gender, or sexual orientation outside majority culture. Recent work in cognitive-perceptual theory has demonstrated that personality—and the social construction of personhood in which it is often implicated—fundamentally shapes which experiences, events, and memories we chose to remember or recognize. The complexities of the gendered speaking self have been the subject of considerable study in recent decades by theorists such as Sidonie Smith, Julia Watson, Leigh Gilmore, and Felicity Nussbaum, who have argued that the stories women tell of their own lives and experiences often reveal a particularly complicated negotiation between multiple selves and multiple layers of the self. Speaking in particular about the rather drab domestic lives of British travelers Isabella Bird and Mary Kingsley, for example, Susan Bassnett observes that "the woman at home appears barely recognizable as the woman abroad" (10); it was travel itself that afforded "the space necessary for them to assert themselves" (11), to re-fashion themselves and their life stories as assertive, inquisitive, and adventurous.

Perhaps most importantly for the study of the travel narratives considered in this volume, Nussbaum illustrates in her book *The Autobiographical Subject: Gender and Ideology in Eighteenth-Century England* that the emergence of middle-class women's life writing in the eighteenth century shaped British culture and politics in fundamental ways. Unsurprisingly, the rise of women's biography and autobiography coincides with the commercial explosion of women's travel writing in the eighteenth century, a period that produced early classics in the genre such as Lady Mary Montagu's Turkish embassy letters and Mary Wollstonecraft's *Letters Written during a Short Residence in Norway, Sweden, and Denmark* (1796).

The very fact of a commercial publishing industry had its own effects on the development of travel writing and on the ways in which the speaking subject represented his or her experiences abroad. Insofar as travel writers imagined that they were writing for an audience within their own home culture, they also constructed that audience for themselves and in their narratives as more like them than not. If our travel writers were, perhaps, willing to acknowledge that they were richer, luckier, or more daring than their average countryman or woman, they also imagined readers who would be interested in and ignorant of many of the same things that they had recently encountered as travelers. Aware that those at home are curious about the foreign and exotic and that their readers share certain pervasive cultural biases against, for example, "heathenism," these writers consciously or unconsciously tailored their accounts to speak to the concerns of their (often commercial) readership. Although there is in travel writing (as in autobiography) a rhetorical imperative to set down a truthful account of the journey, there is also pressure to recount a rollicking adventure. In the interests of immediacy and narrative pacing, travel writers conventionally reconstructed or invented dialogue that cast the authorial self as more intelligent, crafty, ill-treated, exasperated, or perplexed than he or she may "really" have been. Working in what Percy Adams has called a simultaneously documentary and fictional genre, travel writers selected and privileged certain narrative details and words over others in order to intensify the dramatic or comic effect of their prose and assumed that their readers would sanction this narrative license—the same narrative license that is, in fact, inescapable in any life writing.

Even when the account was derived from a diary that was ostensibly not destined for publication, the rhetoric of selection is evident. As Felicity Nussbaum observes of autobiography: "The diarist pretends simply to transcribe the details of experience, but clearly some events are more important to the narrative 'I' than others" (28). From the essays collected in this book, we discover, for example, the extent to which writers employed predominantly "imaginative" forms such as poetry and short story in order to reflect on the significance of history or to educate readers about the salubrious effects of travel on the development of character. Claiming that the repertoire of narrative techniques available to the travel writer borrow from fiction is not to dismiss their effect as falsehood but to enrich our understanding as scholars of the complex connections between prose readership and writerly choices.

In imagining both their readership and their authorial selves, these writers also struggled with the problems of national identity. With the historical intensification of nationalism in the eighteenth century, the seeing self of the traveler and the encountered world came to be established through conventions of cultural representation, national consciousness, and an incomplete sense of self-knowledge. In some travel accounts, the social and national self collapses into fiction in the face of new experiences. There are tales of travelers "going native," narratives in which the (typically Oriental) other imposes itself upon the voyager, either as educative inflection or as monstrous infection, depending on the degree of cultural contact and interpenetration. These are the stories of Lady Mary Montagu in the harems and baths of Constantinople and those famous images of T. E. Lawrence, in the character of "Lawrence of Arabia," dressed in desert robes. In the context of imperial relations, Edward Said has famously theorized this experience as "hybridity," by which he means to describe the process of self-fashioning that occurs when the observed finds himself or herself taking on the manners, costume, and speech of the other. More often, however, the travel narratives of the eighteenth, nineteenth, and twentieth centuries demonstrate an authorial effort to represent the national self as organic, unified, and stable, even in the face of new and often *personally* transformative experiences. Despite private idiosyncrasies and those "Frances Mayes" moments in which the traveler's most intimate self-perceptions about the direction or meaning of his or her life are altered, the travel writer enacts and performs national identity while abroad, and it is typically a national identity that remains unaltered by foreign experience. We read in the history of Western travel writing remarkably few narratives of defection. This is perhaps, in part, because each traveler carries with him or her certain collectively coded experiences that shape both the perception of the public self and the perception of the foreign other. And perhaps, in part, it is because few readers at home care to imagine an experience of travel that leads to such a radical disintegration of the self. As commentators on the travel writing traditions have often observed, few genres are more concerned with the strategies of narrative desire.

Travel and Narrative Visuality

Perhaps one of the most important insights reaffirmed in this volume, then, is that the self of the traveler is fictionalized in discursive and often consciously literary ways. However, as Mary Louise Pratt argued in her seminal work *Imperial Eyes: Travel Writing and Transculturation*, travel writing has also been historically a genre that employed the technologies of the visible, often in aggressive ways. The seeing eye—often understood as an appropriate synecdoche for the seeing *I*—represented the voyeuristic impulses of the traveler and his or her desire to report scientifically and objectively on experiences that were fundamentally complicated in all the ways that selfhood and self-representation inevitably are. If in the eighteenth and early nineteenth centuries this seeing subject ranged from the imperial eye of the colonialist period to the transparent eyeball of the American transcendentalists, in the later part of the nineteenth century and into the twentieth it is the figure of the urban *flâneur* that most profoundly shaped modern travel and the emergence of contemporary tourism.

Recent critical work in literary studies has established the roving *flâneur* as a predominant metaphorical figure in nineteenth-century culture, one whose presence in a tale sheds light on narrative techniques of visuality. For, more than just a wandering and transparent eye, the *flâneur's* acquisitive stance toward the world defines a type of travel writing in which people and things are appropriated for their exotic nature. Derived especially from the work of nineteenth-century French writer Charles Baudelaire, the figure of the *flâneur* is particularly important to twentieth-century critics, who see in the experiences of this internal wanderer a universality that speaks to the presence of travel and mobility in modern urban life. In Walter Benjamin's *Arcades Project*, for example, his *flâneur* walks the city, and in his movements layers of history and meaning unfold: "[t]he street conducts the *flâneur* into a vanished time" (416). Perhaps most importantly, Benjamin's work hints at the more direct relationship between the *flâneur* and the tourist/traveler, emphasizing the centrality of transportation technologies in the imagination of both (428).

Although the *flâneur* is traditionally a male, urban figure, his defining qualities replicate those of many travelers whose works are investigated in this book.[3] Perhaps most essentially, the *flâneur* is bourgeois, one who has the money, leisure, and class distinction to move freely within and across borders. As critics such as James Buzard and Dean MacCannell have argued, the twentieth-century tourist is a relentlessly bourgeois figure, engaged in the acquisition of cultural capital and representing the interests of what MacCannell calls "the new leisure class." The *flâneur* is the modern tourist's immediate predecessor. Like this new leisure class, the *flâneur* does not typically travel out of necessity but, rather, from a need to fuel his desire for pleasure and experience. And, not coincidentally, like the camera-toting hoards that descend each year on the capital cities of the West and tropical island paradises around the world, the pleasures of the *flâneur* are predominantly visual. To the *flâneur*, the city is a canvas upon which the richness and diversity of urban life are painted. References to painters, ways of seeing, and the intense visual quality of the city are essential, for example, to Baudelaire's concept of the *flâneur* as a visionary:

> We might also liken him to a mirror as vast as the crowd itself; or to a kaleidoscope endowed with consciousness, which, with each one of its movements, represents the multiplicity of life and the flickering grace of all the elements of life. (Baudelaire, *L'Art romantique*, qtd. Benjamin 443)

Throughout the cultural tradition surrounding the figure, the attitude of the *flâneur* is a consciously adopted stance taken toward the world, one that emphasizes the visual or reflective nature of the modern capitalist self. As such, the *flâneur* represents one of a series of textual personas available to travelers, one that has become, with the rise of commercial tourism, increasingly prevalent.

This is not, of course, to suggest that other historical models of travel did not significantly inflect the rise of the tourist as culture figure. Certainly, the archetype of the colonial traveler and his "imperial eyes" also persists as an important component of the contemporary rhetoric of travel. Once again, however, these are representations that emphasize the same visuality at the heart of the *flâneur*. The legacy of the colonial traveler is so strong that it has shaped popular perceptions of "the traveler" in visual media ranging from film and television to advertising. In twentieth-century film, there is the khaki-clad elegance of Ralph Fiennes in *The English Patient*, Harrison Ford as the now-archetypal Indiana Jones in *Raiders of the Lost Ark*, Tom Selleck in *High Road to China*, and Michael Douglas in *Romancing the Stone*. That these travelers are male, English, and American, however, is significant. Charismatic mavericks who speak the language of the natives, these male travelers are untroubled by their singular position in the world of the other. Their qualities are physical strength, charm, resourcefulness, and an adroit ability to resist the corruption of the environment—and they make quick use of a weapon. Even Paul Fussell plays with this identity in his influential study *Abroad: British Literary Traveling Between the Wars*. As he laments the decline of travel and the rise of tourism, he recounts his travel fantasy of an excursion to the South Pacific, drawn from the pages of Somerset Maugham: "I saw myself lolling at the rail unshaven in a dirty white linen suit as the crummy little ship approached Bora Boara or Fiji in a damp heat which made one wonder whether death by yaws or dengue fever might be an attractive alternative" (41). This archetype of the gentleman traveler in crumpled linen is clearly shaped by the imaginative power of colonial exploration and settlement.

Mapping the Voyage Out

As we have suggested, these themes and questions are at the heart of the essays that follow, and the collection begins in Chapter Two with Valerie Smith's reflections on a contemporary travel narrative, Rebecca Solnit's *A Book of Migrations* (1998), a work ostensibly about contemporary Ireland that reveals Solnit's attempts to come to terms with her Irish heritage. As Smith demonstrates, Solnit's work is travel narrative as "cultural autobiography," a text in which the author interpolates history, autobiography, and travel in order to articulate a definition of national identity. In this regard, Solnit's book reflects the broader shift in twentieth-century travel writing away from the genre's earlier documentary impulses. If the typical travel narrative of the nineteenth century was a scientific text addressed to professional colleagues, purveying useful information for the colonialist project, recent accounts track an individual writer's "responses or consciousness" in response to place (Carr 74). While readers learn about the country of Ireland from her writing, they also learn about Solnit's predispositions and attitudes, about the habits of mind that shape her written word. Departing from a Modernist perspective of alienation that posits the relative stability of the self, Solnit's quest to understand and define "the Irish" for herself and for her readers reveals that identity is liminal, fluctuating between the personal and the national and often realized in outward cultural artifacts such as film.

Smith's essay on Solnit demonstrates that lived experience is often inseparable from textual experience, and this relationship between life and art is further explored and problematized in Jeanne Dubino's contribution to this book in Chapter Three. Dubino demonstrates the extent to which autobiographical works depend on nostalgia and cultural commodities for structure and meaning. American author Melinda Atwood moved to Kenya, built a home, raised her son, and lived in the country for six years. She recorded her experiences and later published them as *Jambo, Mama* (2001). As Dubino observes, however, the resulting written work depends heavily on Karen Blixen's *Out of Africa* (1937) for its tone, its vision of African life, and its construction of the female colonial self. Blixen's work is the template for Atwood's book, and her account is further mediated by the filmed version of *Out of Africa* (1985), starring Meryl Streep and Robert Redford, which offers Atwood stylized constructions of the colonial self that she liberally invokes in order to craft her authorial persona. Despite recent criticism linking the romance of colonialism directly to the ideologies of race and empire, the imperialist is powerfully alluring to Atwood, whose work demonstrates the extent to which the legacy of European expansion into Africa is softened—if not elided—by the cultural memory of film and literature.

In his essay "Firebrand and the Cat" (Chapter Four), Russ Pottle also illuminates the complexity of self-fashioning and the development of textual identity and to important rhetorical effect. In the case of his subject, the colonialist English landowner and surveyor William Byrd, more than one textual identity was fashioned by the traveler. Byrd composed his *History of the Dividing Line betwixt Virginia and North Carolina* in a style and form addressed to his natural-science colleagues in London and crafts in the text a consciously public and formal persona. At the same time, however, Byrd was also writing a parallel text, the *Secret History of the Line*, a satirical text intended for "an intimate circle of readers" (Pottle), in which he is gossipy, splenetic, and far more candid. Pottle's analysis of these divergent texts and authorial personas argues for the constructed nature of documentary accounts both of history and of the self.

In Chapter Five, Shoshannah Ganz casts further light on the question of intertextuality and autobiography in her detailed study of the 1940 poem of pilgrimage, *Brébeuf and His Brethren*. E. J. Pratt's poem was inspired by the story of the perilous experiences of seventeenth-century Jesuits in Canada, who had established a mission near what is today Midland, Ontario. Sympathetic to and friendly with the Huron, the priests fell afoul of the Iroquois, who captured and tortured them. In the early twentieth century, a shrine was erected near the site of the old mission, and archeological work began to uncover Brébeuf's grave and significant artifacts from in the area. Pratt began researching the life of Brébeuf to lend historical and topographical accuracy to his commemorative poem, relying heavily on the records of missions compiled in the *Jesuit Relations* (1632-1673) and on the work of nineteenth-century scholar Pelham Edgar. Yet, as Ganz reveals, despite the painstaking historical research, the work represents a personal journey of faith and is inflected by the same strategies of storytelling and allusion that make the site a popular Christian tourist destination in the present moment.

In Chapter Six, Clare McCotter considers seafaring as a symbol for self-construction and colonial encounter in travel writing, and, focusing on the rhetoric of the voyage out particularly, McCotter argues that, for Irish travel writer Beatrice Grimshaw, the boat becomes a metaphor for exploring and testing domestic relations and gender stereotypes. Taking a psychoanalytic approach, McCotter encourages us to read Grimshaw's writing for the experiences of liminality and self-construction embodied in the text.

In Chapter Seven, Sarah Wadsworth's essay "Travel Reading and Travel Writing in Louisa May Alcott's 'Poppies and Wheat'" explores the instructive qualities of American writer Louisa May Alcott's short fiction and its relationship to autobiographical travel writing. Wadsworth demonstrates that Alcott's didacticism deliberately employed the figure of an idealized traveler throughout her short-story collection *A Garland for Girls* (1888). At the same time, the stories have a simultaneously autobiographical and commercial aspect. In 1865 and 1866, Alcott had traveled to Europe as a companion to a wealthy young American woman, and her short story "Poppies and Wheat" fictionalizes her experiences and observations while employing her celebrity status as an author. Contrasting the characters of the flighty "Ethel" and thoughtful, less-privileged "Jenny," Alcott provides her readers with a model of self-improvement that centers on the educative effects of travel as an occasion for historical, aesthetic, and moral study.

As the writers collected in this volume demonstrate, travel writing embodies the richness of physical adventure and personal self-discovery while celebrating the familiarity of the beaten path and, throughout the modern era, the pleasures of acquiring cultural capital. Sometimes the acquisition of that cultural capital has served purposes of which it is important to be critical—purposes of colonialism, conquest, and domination of different sorts. And yet, as these writers also show, in some instances learning to see the world and to see oneself differently as a result of the encounter, however limited historically and culturally that perception may be, also results in a kind of education that is intimately connected to the very idea of the Western self and that mobilizes the permeability of the inner and the outer, the discourse of self as voyage.

Notes

[1] As James Buzard observes in *The Beaten Track* (1993), by the nineteenth century certain itineraries that had once represented a mode of exploration had become just that—itineraries, mapped and predictable spaces that became part of a familiar model of cultural reproduction and consumption.

[2] On the relationship between travel writing and autobiography, see especially Ineke Bockting (1998), Lloyd Davis (2003), Vesna Goldsworthy (2000), and Richard van Leeuwen (1998).

[3] Scholars debate the possibility of the female *flâneur* or *flâneuse*. See works by Rachel Bowlby (1992), Dana Brand (1991), Anne Friedberg (1993), Chris Jenks (1995), Deborah Parsons (2000), Griselda Pollock (1988), Erika Rappaport (1999), Keith Tester (1994), Judith Walkowitz (1992), Elizabeth Wilson (1992), and Janet Wolff (1989).

Works Cited

Adams, Percy. *Travelers and Travel Liars, 1660-1800*. Berkeley: U of California P, 1962.

Alcott, Louisa May. *A Garland for Girls.* 1888. New York: Grosset & Dunlap, 1908.

Atwood, Melinda. *Jambo, Mama*. Ft. Bragg, CA: Cypress House, 2000.

Barthes, Roland. "An Introduction to the Structural Analysis of Narrative." *New Literary History* 6.2 (Winter 1975): 237-72.

Bassnett, Susan. "The Empire, Travel Writing, and British Studies." *Travel Writing and the Empire*. Ed. Sachindananda Mohanty. New Dehli: Katha, 2003. 1-21.

Baudelaire, Charles. *Paris Spleen*. 1869. Trans. Louise Varèse. New York: New Directions, 1970.

Benjamin, Walter. *The Arcades Project*. Trans. Howard Eiland and Kevin McLaughlin. Cambridge, MA: Belknap P, 1999.

Blanton, Casey. *Travel Writing: The Self and the World*. New York: Twayne, 1997.

Bockting, Ineke. "Travel Writing as Autobiography: The Case of Eddy L. Harris." *Writing Lives: American Biography and Autobiography*. Ed. Hans Bak and Hans Krabbendam. Amsterdam, Netherlands: Vrije Universiteit Press, 1998. 146-55.

Bowlby, Rachel. *Still Crazy After All These Years*. New York: Routledge, 1992.

Brand, Dana. *The Spectator and the City in Nineteenth-Century American Literature*. New York: Cambridge UP, 1991.

Buzard, James. *The Beaten Track: European Tourism, Literature, and the Ways to Culture, 1800-1918*. New York: Oxford UP, 1993.

Byron, George Gordon, Lord. *Works of Lord Byron: Letters and Journals*. Ed. Rowland E. Prothero. 12 vols. New York: Octagon, 1966.

Carr, Helen. "Modernism and Travel (1880-1940)." *The Cambridge Companion to Travel Writing*. Ed. Peter Hulme and Tim Youngs. New York: Cambridge UP, 2002. 70-86.

Davis, Lloyd. "Self-Representation and Travel Autobiographies in Early Modern England." *Mapping the Self: Space, Identity, Discourse in British Auto/Biography*. Ed. Frédéric Regard. Saint-Etienne, France: Université de Saint-Etienne, 2003. 55-71.

Dinesen, Isak. *Out of Africa*. 1937. New York: Random House, 1965.

English Patient, The. Dir. Anthony Minghella. With Ralph Fiennes, Juliette Binoche, Kirsten Scott Thomas, and Willem Dafoe. Miramax, 1996.

Friedberg, Anne. "The Mobilized and Virtual Gaze in Modernity: *Flâneur/Flâneuse*." *Window Shopping: Cinema and the Postmodern*. Berkeley: U California P, 1993.

Fussell, Paul. *Abroad: British Literary Traveling Between the Wars*. New York: Oxford UP, 1980.

Gilmore, Leigh. *Autobiographics: A Feminist Theory of Women's Self-Representation*. Ithaca: Cornell UP, 1994.

Goldsworthy, Vesna. "Travel Writing as Autobiography: Rebecca West's Journey of Self-Discovery." *Representing Lives: Women and*

Auto/Biography. Ed. Alison and Pauline Polkey. New York: Macmillan; St. Martin's, 2000.

Grewal, Inderpal. *Home and Harem: Nation, Gender, Empire, and the Cultures of Travel*. Durham, NC: Duke UP, 1996.

Grimshaw, Beatrice. *In The Strange South Seas*. London: Hutchinson & Co., 1907.

"Ground Zero Renewal Features Green Building, Open Space." *Environmental News Service* 6 May 2004 *[New York, NY]*. 26 Sep. 2006 <http://www.ens-newswire.com/ens/may2004/2004-05-06-01.asp>.

Harper, Lila Marz. *Solitary Travelers: Nineteenth-Century Women's Travel Narratives and the Scientific Vocation*. Madison, NJ: Fairleigh Dickinson UP, 2001.

High Road to China. Dir. Brian Hutton. With Tom Selleck and Bess Armstrong. City Films, Golden Harvest Company Ltd., Jadran Film, Pan Pacific Productions, 1983.

Jenks, Chris. "Watching Your Step: The History and Practice of the *Flâneur*." *Visual Culture*. Ed. Chris Jenks. New York: Routledge, 1995.

Lawrence, Karen. *Penelope Voyages: Women and Travel in the British Literary Tradition*. Ithaca, NY: Cornell UP, 1994.

Leeuwen, Richard van. "Autobiography, Travelogue and Identity." *Writing the Self: Autobiographical Writing in Modern Arabic Literature*. Ed. Robin Ostle, Ed de Moor, and StefanWild. London: Saqi, 1998. 27-29.

Lisle, Debbie. "Gazing at Ground Zero: Tourism, Voyeurism and Spectacle." *Journal for Cultural Research* 8.1 (January 2004): 3-21.

Leed, Eric. *The Mind of the Traveler: From Gilgamesh to Global Tourism*. New York: Basic Books, 1991.

MacCannell Dean. *The Tourist: A New Theory of the Leisure Class*. Berkeley: U California P, 1999.

Marcus, Laura. *Auto/biographical Discourses: Theory, Criticism, Practice*. Manchester: Manchester UP, 1994.

Mohanty, Chandra Talpade. "Under Western Eyes: Feminist Scholarship and Colonial Discourses." *Third World Women and the Politics of Feminism*. Ed. Chandra Mohanty, Ann Russo, and Lourdes Torres. Indianapolis: Indiana UP, 1991.

Montagu, Mary Wortley, Lady. 1716. *The Turkish Embassy Letters*. Ed. Anita Desai. London: Virago, 1994.

Nussbaum, Felicity. *The Autobiographical Subject: Gender and Ideology in Eighteenth-Century England*. Baltimore, MD: Johns Hopkins UP, 1989.

Out of Africa. Dir. Sydney Pollack. With Robert Redford, Meryl Streep, and Klaus Maria Brandauer. Universal Studios, 1985.

"Outrage at Ground Zero Visitor Platform." *BBC News*. 17 Jan. 2002. BBC. 26 Sep. 2006 <http://news.bbc.co.uk/1/hi/world/americas/1766687.stm>.

Parsons, Deborah. *Streetwalking the Metropolis: Women, the City, and Modernity*. New York: Oxford UP, 2000.

Pollock, Griselda. "Modernity and the Spaces of Femininity." *Vision and Difference*. London: Routledge, 1988.

Pratt, E[dwin]. J[ohn]. *Brébeuf and His Brethren*. Toronto, Macmillan Co. of Canada Ltd., 1940.

Pratt, Mary Louise. *Imperial Eyes: Travel Writing and Transculturation*. New York: Routledge, 1992.

Raiders of the Lost Ark. Dir. Steven Spielberg. With Harrison Ford and Sean Connery. Paramount, 1981.

Rappaport, Erika. *Shopping for Pleasure: Women in the Making of London's West End*. Princeton, NJ: Princeton UP, 1999.

Ricouer, Paul. *Oneself as Another*. Chicago: U of Chicago P, 1992.

Rojek, Chris and John Urry. *Touring Cultures: Transformations of Travel and Theory*. New York: Routledge, 1997.

Romancing the Stone. Dir. Robert Zemeckis. With Michael Douglas, Kathleen Turner, and Danny DeVito. Twentieth Century Fox, 1984.

Rose, Gillian. *Feminism and Geography: The Limits of Geographical Knowledge*. Minneapolis: U of Minnesota P, 1993.

Said, Edward. *Orientalism*. New York: Pantheon Books, 1978.

Smith, Sidonie and Julia Watson, eds. *Women, Autobiography, Theory: A Reader*. Madison: U of Wisconsin Press, 1998.

Solnit, Rebecca. *A Book of Migrations: Some Passages in Ireland*. London: Verso, 1997.

Stöckl, Andrea. "Ethnography, Travel Writing and the Self: Reflections on Socially Robust Knowledge and the Authorial Ego." *Forum Qualitative Sozialforschung / Forum: Qualitative Social Research* 7.2 (Feb. 2006): Art. 11. 29 Jun. 2006 <http://www.qualitative-research.net/fqs-texte/2-06/06-2-11-e.htm>.

Spadora, Brian. "A Vacation to Remember: Tourists Made a Pilgrimage to Ground Zero." *Herald News* 9 Sep. 2005 *[Passaic County, NJ]*: A01.

Tester, Keith. *The Flâneur*. New York: Routledge, 1994.

Thoreau, Henry David. *The Maine Woods*. 1864. Ed. Joseph J. Moldenhauer. Princeton: Princeton UP, 1972.

—. *Walden*. Ed. J. Lyndon Shanley. 1854. Princeton: Princeton UP, 1971.

Walkowitz, Judith. *City of Dreadful Delight: Narratives of Sexual Danger in Late Victorian London*. Chicago: University of Chicago Press, 1992.

Watson, Julia, and Sidonie Smith. *De/Colonizing the Subject: The Politics of Gender in Women's Autobiography*. Minneapolis: U of Minnesota P, 1992.

Wilson, Elizabeth. "The Invisible *Flâneur*." *New Left Review* 191 (1992): 90-110.

Wolff, Janet. "The Invisible *Flâneuse*." *The Problems of Modernity: Adorno and Benjamin*. Ed. Andrew Benjamin. New York: Routledge, 1989.

Wollstonecraft, Mary. *Letters Written During a Short Residence in Sweden, Norway, and Denmark*. London: J. Johnson, 1796.

Woolf, Virginia. *The Voyage Out*. London: Duckworth, 1915.

Wordsworth, William. *Guide to the English Lakes*. Oxford: Oxford UP, 1977.

CHAPTER TWO

REBECCA SOLNIT'S *A BOOK OF MIGRATIONS*: *SOME PASSAGES IN IRELAND*, CULTURAL AUTOBIOGRAPHY THROUGH THE DISCOURSE OF DISCOMFORT

VALERIE M. SMITH

Rebecca Solnit opens her 1997 travel narrative, *A Book of Migrations: Some Passages in Ireland*, by declaring "my purple passport with its golden harp seems less like a birthright than a slim book on the mythologies of blood, heritage, and emigration" (vii), thus clearly signaling her willingness to problematize essentialist formulations of identity. Solnit then spends a large part of her narrative troubling and troubled by both biological and cultural notions of ethnic and national identity. Identity theorist Anthony D. Smith argues that "[p]raised or reviled, the nation shows few signs of being transcended, and nationalism does not appear to be losing any of its explosive popular power and significance" (170), but I would argue that Solnit's text exposes important tensions surrounding currently available conceptions of national identity formulations.[1] Solnit's desire to trouble overtly conceptions of identity illuminates nuanced social concerns and anxieties about the legitimacy of existing identity formulations, and the contradictions which emerge from her text expose the stress-lines and boundaries that mark contemporary struggles to imagine, or re-imagine, alternative formulations of identity.

Solnit also spends much of her preface firmly positioning herself as anything but an authority on Ireland, thereby signaling her awareness of the problematics of cultural representation within the travel narrative. Solnit begins by announcing "[t]his is not a book about Ireland so much as it is a book about a journey through Ireland," then "hasten[s] to disclaim any great authority on the subjects of Irish history and culture" (vii). As if still troubled that readers may misconstrue her intentions, she further asserts, "this is no core sample of contemporary Ireland; in the same spirit Irish tourists may head straight for Graceland, I took off for the places that appealed to me and let attractions and invitations stitch together the rest of my route" (vii). In reiterating her awareness of the problematics of cultural representation within the travel narrative in this deliberate manner, Solnit moves beyond signaling mere consciousness of a problem to self-consciously exposing her struggles as a travel writer grappling with tricky ethical issues. In order to signal further her understanding that readers may approach travel narratives with certain expectations, she carefully promises, toward the close of her preface, that "[t]his book is itself not a travel book in the usual sense" (viii). Her avowal, which clearly rests upon what she considers genre-conventions, establishes her conscious decision not to work within those conventions.[2] The "discourse of discomfort" that repeats itself throughout Solnit's text consciously and self-consciously focuses on problems of reception, audience expectation, and the travel writer's ethical responsibilities, but Solnit's narrative does not rest there. *A Book of Migrations* weaves an intricate, multidirectional consideration of history, empire, and the impact of globalization[3] through its often less-than-comfortable, highly self-conscious exploration of identity politics and travel, thereby chronicling an important moment of contemporary "cultural autobiography."

"Cultural autobiography," in brief, is the story of the cultural concerns and anxieties that emerge from travel narratives which expose or illuminate entrenched values and ideological assumptions—and the tensions that surround them—from multiple directions.[4] Rebecca Solnit's narrative reveals nuanced cultural concerns and anxieties through its self-conscious construction of a narrative persona, its representation of other peoples and cultures within asymmetrical relations of power, its consideration of identity politics, and through the slippages that surface in spite of its overtly announced ethical stance. In spite of Solnit's careful production of a narrative persona engaged in the "discourse of discomfort" and her troubling of conceptions of identity and the relationship between tourism and imperialism, Solnit's narrative ultimately remains unable to move beyond the necessity of establishing markers, based upon biological formulations, to re-legitimize national identity. The significant limitations Solnit's narrative reveals in its consideration of identity from multiple directions allow us to explore crucial contemporary stresses surrounding the intersections of ethnic and national identity, travel, travel writing, and imperialism, globalization and the epistemology of modernity. On a more local level, Solnit struggles to find a solution to the conundrum of national identity for Americans in an era in which tensions between multiculturalism and assimilation are raising increasingly complex issues.

What I call the "discourse of discomfort" is a system of discourse that deliberately engages in the conscious and self-conscious troubling of social and ethical issues within the unique framework provided by the nonfiction travel narrative. As the study of the travel narrative has grown, so has, I would argue, an overt awareness of the ethics of cultural representation on the part of travel writers.[5] Solnit's travel narrative is unusual in that it explicitly cites several theorists whose work has helped to provide an apparatus for problematizing the representation of other peoples and cultures in textual accounts.[6] Solnit's early references to the works of Dean MacCannell and Edward Said deliberately highlight her awareness of the ethical dimensions implicit in the acts of travel and tourism and in the production of written accounts that represent peoples and cultures. Solnit's careful production of the discourse of discomfort through her engagement with travel theory collides with her more stock representations of Ireland and the Irish, which reflect ideological assumptions based upon more essentialist conceptions of identity. What ultimately emerges from Solnit's work is a map of the vexed borders that contain contemporary concerns about the legitimacy of national identity: what can be said and why and what still remains unspeakable even within narratives that attempt to interrogate such limits.

As part of her project, Solnit's narrative recognizes and deliberately troubles ethical issues surrounding what Dean MacCannell calls the "unifying consciousness" of modernity. Modernity, as defined by MacCannell, results in a view of the modern world as "alienating, wasteful, violent, superficial, unplanned, unstable and inauthentic" (2), but it also results in an impulse for control, a desire to conquer all unindustrialized worlds and imbue them with the unifying consciousness of modernity (3). "Moderns" (those who live in industrialized nations for these purposes) believe that the modern world is corrupt, competitive, exploitative, amoral, meaningless, and alienating. One solution to the disaffection experienced by moderns is to seek spiritual renewal by traveling to more "authentic" regions, such as Ireland, as Irish tourism theorist Barbara O'Connor notes in her discussion of "Myths and Mirrors: Tourist Images and National Identity" (72-73). While Solnit's narrator decries "New Agers" who search for spiritual renewal with their parasitical relationship to other cultures, her own touristic spiritual quest, as she searches for answers to alternative formulations of national and ethnic identity in Ireland, certainly seems to belie the distinctions she wants to make between herself and New Agers and consciously recognizes as uncomfortably less than merited. As Solnit admits, "Perhaps I shouldn't say too much about the [International Transpersonal Psychology Association] conference or its audience. It may be that the flocks of New Age followers annoy me because in some ways I resemble them" (89). In recognizing her similarities to those whom she would criticize, Solnit exposes her awareness of her own embeddedness within the structures of tourism and imperialism, in spite of her ethical condemnation of those structures. In signaling her discomfort with the apparently limited positions available, Solnit's narrative exposes strengths and weaknesses in the ideological assumptions that construct and constrict the epistemology of identity for moderns.

Solnit first announces the "quest" upon which she is bound, thus revealing her own desire for "spiritual renewal" through travel to more "authentic" regions, in her preface, when she declares "Ireland delighted me by offering so many stories and circumstances in which individuals and populations were fluid rather than ossified, undermining the usual travelers' dichotomy of a mobile figure in an immobile landscape. It was this play between memory, identity, movement, and landscape that I wanted to explore, and the ebb and flow of populations that constitutes invasion, exile, colonization, emigration, tourism, and nomadism" (vii). In making such a statement, Solnit positions Ireland as offering a unique setting through which to "explore" her concerns; Ireland as place serves Solnit's modernist needs by providing an appropriate environment in which to seek answers. She further explains her quest when she remarks, "I wanted to think in a different landscape about questions that had arisen for me in my own: about the concentric circles of identity formed by memory, the body, the family; by the community, tribe or ethnic group; by locale, nationality, language and literature—and about the wild tides that have washed over those neat circles, tides of invasion, colonization, emigration, exile, nomadism, and tourism" (7). Her description of the questions that have impelled her trip, along with her desire to consider them "in a different landscape," implies an understanding of particular types of landscape as somehow more capable of providing answers to her questions. Solnit then rounds out the description of her quest by explaining that "new and unknown places called forth strange, oft-forgotten correspondences and desires in the mind, so that the motion of travel takes place as much in the psyche as anywhere else. Travel offers the opportunity to find out who else one is, in that collapse of identity into geography I want to trace" (7). Solnit's desire to find out "who else" she is outside the structure provided by the familiar landscapes of modern, industrialized society clearly situates her within the framework of the spiritual quest, in spite of her equally clear ethical discomfort with such a framework.

Questions surrounding identity formations and formulations, definitions of "who else one is," become more urgent as the tensions between nationalism and globalization produce both centrifugal and centripetal pressures. Increasing globalization often requires new, contradictory conceptions of citizenship, but, as Smith notes, "[n]ationalism provides perhaps the most compelling identity myth in the modern world" (viii). Whether we work under what Smith terms a "Western" model of identity in which individuals have to "belong to some nation but [can] choose to which [they] belong," or under a "non-Western or ethnic concept," in which "[w]hether you stayed in your community or emigrated to another, you remained ineluctably, organically, a member of the community of your birth and were forever stamped by it" (11), we will almost always find ourselves bumping up against contradictions within the models, as does Solnit, especially if we interrogate their underpinnings. Smith's "Western" model is based upon ideas surrounding the cultural construction of identity and the value of assimilation; his "non-Western" model is based upon biological or essentialist concepts of identity, neither of which is an entirely comfortable fit for Solnit, yet neither of which she can entirely escape, just as she cannot entirely escape the epistemological framework of modernism. Even if we think of nations and national identity, in the sense in which they exist today, as relatively modern constructs, as do most historians, dating their emergence to anywhere between the eighteenth and the twentieth centuries, it is difficult to view ourselves outside the system of discourse that constructs us as nationals—yet increasing globalization often demands we do just that. I use the term "globalization" here as a means through which to consider one increasingly visible aspect around which identity is becoming re-imagined.[7] The freshness of the air we breath, the purity and availability of the water we drink, the spread and treatment of disease, the unprecedented movements of peoples across the globe, and the transnational nature of the global economy are all reliant upon more than national conceptions of identity, yet conceptions of national identity still appear prevalent.[8] While one aspect of the identity axis demands that we imagine ourselves beyond national boundaries, another aspect demands that we continue to imagine ourselves within those national boundaries, and yet another aspect trains our focus toward ethnic conceptions of identity.

One of the most important stories that emerges from Solnit's travel narrative is the story of the constraints and contradictions through which the United States is attempting to re-imagine itself in a global era as it struggles with the centripetal and centrifugal forces outlined above. Part of this story revolves around Solnit's struggles with trying to re-imagine an ethnic identity. The problem occurs when Solnit attempts to interrogate the "myth" of national identity while remaining within the structure of the myth, and the ideological framework of modernity is exposed both in the discomfort she posits over her "purple passport" and in her troubled explanation of her "ethnic" identity. She describes herself as a "third-generation Irish-American," but then immediately qualifies that with "I'm not much of an Irishwoman, let alone a Catholic, since my father's parents were immigrant Russian Jews, and I've been in hybrid California, world capital of amnesia, nearly all my life" (6). It seems there is no one place from which Solnit can comfortably speak *about* the forces that are assumed to produce ethnic identity—they are too contradictory to produce a coherent narrative—yet the modernist epistemological framework desires unification. Solnit displays her awareness of many of the complex issues surrounding the imagination of ethnic identity through the discourse of discomfort in which she engages, as well as through her conscious construction of an anti-sentimental narrative persona, which she early on and quite vigorously adopts as if to deliberately combat any stereotypical image of Irish-American sentimentality her audience may be expecting.

Even though some historians would argue that Irish Americans had important advantages in terms of their eventual social acceptance,[9] early anti-Irish nativism resulted in the proliferation of such virulent stereotypes as "drunkenness, ignorance, laziness, moral laxity, idolatry, political indoctrination" (Kenny 117). In his discussion of *The American Irish*, historian Kevin Kenny theorizes that, although originally lacking "any well-defined sense of national, as distinct from regional or local, identity," the Irish, as did many immigrant groups, eventually developed a more coherent sense of ethnic identity as part of the process of assimilation (Kenny 148). Instead of stereotypes "hindering assimilation," Kenny argues, "the development of [a previously nonexistent] ethnic identity [through the adaptation of some stereotypes] expressed through a rich institutional and associational life [the result of the need for group cohesion to counterbalance nativist animosity] was the primary means through which the American Irish assimilated" (148-49). In other words, through their organizational life, the American Irish adopted an ethnic identity by which they found a means of cultural assimilation. Maureen Dezell implies agreement with Kenny's argument in *Irish America: Coming into Clover*, in which she claims that

> American popular culture by the 1900s had embraced the idea that the Irish were a genial, down-to-earth, self-effacing people with a romantic past and a weakness for drink. For better and for worse, so had the Irish—which is why those notions define Irish America's image and self-image to this day. [. . .] Descendents of dreamers and tale-tellers in the land of money, myth, and Disney, the American Irish early on developed a capacity for romanticizing their heritage and sentimentalizing themselves[.] (18).

It was this sentimentality, Dezell further argues, that "became Irish America's signature style" (24). This "style" allowed Irish Americans to scoop out a relatively unthreatening niche for themselves in the stewpot of assimilation,[10] but not one without lingering repercussions.

Because of the greater degree of at least superficial assimilation experienced by many Irish Americans, Solnit's narrative is freer to move beyond the pressures and boundaries faced by many other ethnic American writers. Even so, *A Book of Migrations* is, in some sense, still locked within and limited by an ongoing conversation about the markers of Irish ethnicity. Solnit's careful construction of an anti-sentimental persona, which she first establishes through her affinity to Jonathon Swift, signals her awareness of some of the lingering tensions felt in contemporary Irish America over continuing stereotypes. Solnit points out that "More than half a million of Ireland's annual visitors are US reverse immigrants, coming to look at where their ancestors came from," finally complaining that "One of the ineffable byproducts of these touristic transactions is sentimentality" (15). She notes that she rejects such sentimentality herself ("it's what made going to Ireland such a dubious adventure for me" [15]) and continues to cite those things that make Ireland "insufferably cute in the popular American imagination [. . .] shamrocks, Lucky Charms breakfast cereal, green beer on St Patrick's Day, lines of syrupy old songs like 'When Irish Eyes Are Smiling,' and sticky catch-phrases like 'the auld sod'" (15). To counteract this sentimentality, Solnit's narrator reports that she goes in search of "the tomb of one of the most publicly unsentimental men in European history, Jonathan Swift" (15). While she admits "I too was a tourist in Ireland" (16), she actively sets herself apart from her fellow reverse immigrants by aligning herself with Swift, noting that "the question of whether he was English or Irish was and is answered according to desire and politics rather than any clear cut fact. It might be most accurate to say he was both. [. . .] He seems to have been something of an exile wherever he was, not wholly a member of either country, split between comfort and conscience" (17). Solnit's determination to combat stereotypes of the Irish through her alignment with Swift and her construction of a deliberately anti-sentimental persona points to the cultural capital such stereotypes still possess and to the epistemological limits her engagement with complex formulations of identity can go.

In one of her anti-sentimental discussions about identity, Solnit signals her rejection of sentimental notions of racial purity by noting that "Even Irish identity depends as much on forgetting as on remembering, on forgetting that the Celts were not always Irish and the Irish were not always Celts, on forgetting that for all the conservative, stubborn tradition, they have also changed drastically again and again since the days when they were pastoralist tribes" (118). Solnit's focus on flux, rather than stasis, clearly appears to position her as questioning essentialist conceptions of identity formation. She further explains that:

> The rocklike foundation for identity an ancestral land is supposed to be was dissolving before my eyes into a river of transformations. The longer I passed through the Ireland that both the Irish and the Irish-Americans seem to imagine as a solid foundation, the more it seemed instead to be made up of a continuous flow of discontinuities and accelerating movements, of colonizations and decolonizations, liberations, exiles, emigrations, invasions, economic pendulums, developments, abandonments, acculturaltions, simulations. (132)

Solnit unambiguously rejects sentimental notions of essentialist racial purity through her deliberate engagement with the discourse of discomfort and through her focus on Ireland as continuous subject of vast population changes. Yet, in what appears to be a direct contradiction of her anti-sentimental, anti-essentialist position, Solnit adapts a sentimental and nostalgic tone while, in looking regretfully toward the future, she muses, "Another generation should sweep away rural culture, modify Catholicism, assimilate to the European community and the global markets and continue to emigrate, and through the hole they widened, the world would come pouring in" (132). While Solnit seems ready to challenge the sentimental notion of origin myths and the assumptions that underlie their ideology within some areas of her narrative, she unquestioningly upholds several romanticized, sentimental conceptions of the Irish as living in a separate, timeless, more "authentic" world, one which verges on the brink of ruin, within other areas of her travel narrative.

In spite of her self-conscious adaptation of a determinedly anti-sentimental persona, Solnit's representation of Ireland and the Irish actually upholds and values many sentimental tourist images of Ireland as a "pre-modern" society. As O'Connor explains in her discussion of tourist imagery, "Ireland is represented as a place of picturesque scenery and unspoiled beauty, of friendly and quaint people, a place which is steeped in past traditions and ways of life. In short it is represented as a pre-modern society" (70). O'Connor further comments that it is this very type of "[t]ourism imagery [that] has been instrumental in constructing Ireland and the Irish people as 'other' to the modern industrial metropolitan centres of Europe and the US" (76). In its iteration of such tourist imagery, Solnit's narrative often focuses on Ireland as a pre-modern, somehow more "authentic," society. Indeed, her discussion of Ireland often veers toward a nostalgic construction of Irish "time" based in the very type of sentimentality she works so forcefully to unravel elsewhere in relation to her construction of an Irish-American self.

In one of her sentimental moves, Solnit's narrator muses on "[d]ream time, clock time, historical time" and claims that "[b]eing in Ireland always seemed like being in some past point of time, sometimes a decade or a half-century ago when it came to oldfashioned customs and unstreamlined ways of doing things, the length of memory and lack of hurry, the occasional horse-drawn cart in Dublin" (144). As O'Connor notes, "[t]ourists are generally coming from a world which is extremely individualistic, fragmented and anonymous. They live in a society which is characterized by highly specific and discontinuing relationships with other people. Simple people who live their lives in traditional ways far from the hurly burly of the city [as the Irish are generally represented in tourist imagery] are sought out as an essential part of the tourist experience" (72). Solnit's sentimental reverie on the timelessness of Ireland certainly appears to fulfill O'Connor's definition of some of the stereotypical experiences tourists expect to undergo while in Ireland—that of escape into a more traditional ("oldfashioned"), authentic ("unstreamlined"), less fragmented ("the length of memory and lack of hurry") "time." In spite of her earlier, troubled discussion of tourism as a form of imperialism ("Tourists have as peculiar an effect on a culture as invaders do," she declares [13]), and her understanding that "tourists most often want an unchanged vision of the past" (13), Solnit's discourse of discomfort entirely disappears during the moments in which her narrator's philosophical musings reveal sentimental "longings" for an escape from the industrialized, modern world. In this case, Solnit's narrator, in spite of her previous declarations about the complexity of national identity and her complaints about tourism as a form of imperialism, seems to offer wholeheartedly the very type of stock national images in her embrace of Ireland's "timelessness" she has previously cautioned against. As Johannes Fabian remarks in *Time and the Other: How Anthropology Makes its Object*, such "distancing devices [. . .] produce [. . .] global [consequences]," which result in a "*denial of coevalness*" or "*a persistent and systematic tendency to place the referent(s) of anthropology in a Time other than the present*" (31). In other words, the use of discourse which constructs cultures as still existing in the past—as somehow "pre-modern" rather than contemporary—reinforces asymmetrical relations of power between modern (superior) nations and timeless (inferior) nations. Solnit's slippage into such discourse, in spite of her avowed awareness of the problematics of cultural representation, reveals yet another direction through which her narrative exposes the limits of disruption within the epistemological framework provided by modernity.

In her discussion of tourists as the latest group to invade Ireland, Solnit begins to signal her dissatisfaction with the intersection of tourism and neo-imperialism by remarking that "[t]here are situations in which tourism can encourage the preservation of a place, but far more frequently, tourists inadvertently stimulate an industry at the cost of the local culture" (13). Solnit then positions herself as critical of "fake authenticity"—that state in which tourist destinations whose "authentic" local cultures are often the draw find themselves—as she positions herself within the discourse of discomfort. She complains that "[t]he vast and ever-expanding industry of tourism threatens to turn the whole world into a series of theaters whose companies perform palatable versions of their culture and history. Tourists thus possess a perverse version of Midas's touch: the authenticity and exoticism they seek is inauthenticated and homogenized by their presence" (14). Yet authenticity, in just this sense, is just what Solnit herself often privileges in her discussion of Ireland when she rhapsodizes on blatantly stock images of cultural "authenticity" in her discussion of Ireland. For example, Ireland's authentic oral culture is juxtaposed with the lack of authentic oral culture elsewhere. Solnit's narrator notes that "no place seems as haunted and infested by stories, and by the past, as Ireland" (50) and admits that "[a]t least for outsiders much of Ireland's charm is that it is still, however literate, an oral [and by implication, more authentic] culture" (51). She rejoices that in Ireland "[t]alk is a principal form of entertainment and an art, and internal memory hasn't been entirely eclipsed by recorded history or amnesia" and bemoans that "[s]tory telling itself has been in a long decline elsewhere, in part because the generations are all but segregated in most industrial societies, because a tale requires a leisurely pace for both teller and listeners, and because telling has been replaced by commercial entertainment," thus openly revealing and almost reveling in her own "modernist longing."[11]

Another aspect of Solnit's modernist epistemology is revealed when she further remarks that "[t]he appetite for stories seems undiminished, but the information and entertainment media have evolved to fill it with narratives in which the listener is forever inaudible and invisible, never the teller or part of the tale. These sources don't really replace firsthand stories, which cast their glow over the events and places of one's own life, incorporate one into a community of meanings" (51). Solnit's sentimental valuation of talking and story telling as more "authentic" forms of communication than "recorded history" or "commercial entertainment," her nostalgic reference to the "glow" they cast and their importance for the formation of community, are quite startling in light of the discourse of discomfort she engages elsewhere in her narrative. She seems to desire the very "unchanged vision of the past" that she has previously derided (13) as ethically suspect in its reproduction of unequal power relations (14). The sentimental images Solnit invokes clearly contribute to the promotion of ideas about national identity as something fixed and classifiable, and they dramatically contradict her discourse of discomfort. Although, on the one hand, Solnit questions origin myths about cultural purity through her problematizing of identity formation, her construction of Ireland as timeless and her privileging of a more authentic (pure) type of communication uphold those very same myths of a more "pure" form of identity to be found in "pre-modern" societies. As O'Connor notes in her discussion of MacCannell, "people in urban capitalist society can feel a superiority over the traditional, at the same time as they seek 'authentic experience' in it—an 'authenticity' which is no longer possible in their everyday life" (77). The tension Solnit's narrative reveals between the ethical desire to problematize notions of cultural superiority through its conscious and self-conscious use of the discourse of discomfort at some moments, and its apparently unconscious adaptation of authenticity as a marker of value elsewhere, uncovers a palpable epistemological barrier to reformulations of identity myths.

When the discourse of discomfort meets the discourse of "modernist longing," contradictions abound. The contradictions I have pointed to between the construction of a Self and the construction of an Other are troubling and complex, but they are not without precedent within the return narrative. What is more unusual is the third position for identity formation offered by Solnit's narrative, in which she argues for an alternative marker of national identity that relies upon a link between biology and territory. It is the tension that emerges as Solnit navigates identity politics through the frame of the travel narrative, which reveals another aspect of the still ubiquitous power of national identity myths, even when a discourse of discomfort about the legitimacy of identity markers is deliberately engaged. This tension is highlighted further when Solnit signals her own discomfort with a perceived lack of easily classifiable identity by regretfully noting that she "[grew] up in a place without a past, the shadeless artifice of suburbia. My parents hardly spoke of their own past, and no one had anything to say of the past of the place we'd landed in" (49-50). Solnit's narrator remorsefully notes that "history hovered outside the borders of my own sedative neighborhood like one of those dreams that are all the more alluring for being just beyond recollection" (50). Although at some moments Solnit's narrator makes it clear that her conception of identity is by no means based in biological bloodlines, she obscures this by highlighting a felt lack of belonging resulting from the inadequacy of those markers "supposed" to define nationality. The lack of a clear sense of "belonging," along with her "longing" for a more solid tie to the past, reveals a complex aspect of the changing face of the assimilation versus multiculturalism debate as the centripetal and centrifugal forces that structure national versus global identity become more visible. To be able to claim an ethnic identity is now more culturally valued then ever before in the United States, as is evidenced in the current (overt) privileging of multiculturalism over assimilation, yet this conflicts, at least in part, with the epistemological demands of imagining global citizenry, as revealed in Solnit's remarks. [12]

"Western" models of identity formulation which value assimilation can result in deeply felt modernist longing and a lack of clear attachment to a particular nation when multicultural models become highly valued. "Non-Western" models, on the other hand, do not fulfill the needs of mobile, highly globalized societies because of their focus on ethnic solidarity. Solnit's narrative actively displays discomfort over the inadequacy of formulations of identity as it exposes tensions between the two models. Solnit's solution to this tension is "bioregionalism," a formulation of identity that relies upon linking biology to territory to re-legitimize notions of national identity.

The alternative formulation of national identity Solnit offers is neither tied to what she sees as the problematic conceptions of ethnic identity raised by "multiculturalism" nor to the inadequate conceptions of cultural identity she sees raised by assimilation. Instead, she proposes a formulation of identity based upon "bioregionalism—a philosophy of coming to belong to one's locale by coming to know and respect its history and nature," a type of "chemistry proposing identity as a compound of ethnicity and geography," which, she is sorry to note, "seems to have fallen out of the conversation as multiculturalism made its entrance" (68). Solnit thus proffers what she sees as a system of identity formation that ties together cultural, biological, and territorial identity to fill a felt void created by the challenges globalization, multiculturalism, assimilation, "invasion, colonization, emigration, exile, nomadism, [and] tourism" (7) pose to what she envisions as more satisfying constructions of national identity. Solnit envisions a more universal construction of national identity by negotiating a middle ground between essentialist and cultural constructions of identity in order to re-legitimize national identity in an era in which it is increasingly under threat.

Solnit provides an example of "bioregionalism" early on in her narrative when she refers to the origin beliefs of some Native Americans, such as the Shoshone, "whose religions often dictate that they were created where they are, with an indissoluble, irreplaceable symbiosis with their landscape" (5). Such origin beliefs, Solnit's narrator explains, have been complicated by scientific findings that the Shoshone were "relatively recent arrivals in the area" (5); such findings are obviously "at odds" with the Shoshone's "sense that they had been here forever, since creation" (5). Solnit's narrator offers a solution to this predicament in which "both versions can be true: the evidence of ancient migrations means one thing, a material history; and the relation of the people to their land means another, a cultural history. As long as their identity is so profoundly situated in their landscape, it is impossible to say that they were people before they were in that landscape" (5). Solnit's narrator's desire to find a "happy medium" in "bioregionalism" accentuates the epistemological struggle to find a tenable solution to contemporary cultural anxieties surrounding identity formation. To demonstrate her willingness to address complications, Solnit's narrator adds that, "[e]ven recognizing the existence of indigenous people in the Americas raises a lot of difficult questions about belonging for those Americans who descend from historical emigrations: questions about what it means to be and whether it's possible to become native; about what kind of a relationship to a landscape and what kind of rootedness it might entail; and about what we can lay claim to at all as the ground of our identity if we are only visitors, travelers, invaders in someone else's homeland" (5). These are questions Solnit answers later in the text, with "[w]hen I think back to my formation, it seems that landscape shaped me, made a home in the truer sense than the centerless house in the subdivision and an identity surer than the vague hints of familial and ethnic history that came my way. I am even literally made of the California landscape, of all the produce, water, wine I have been devouring since I was four" (66-67). The modernist epistemological desire to find an essential spring for national identity formation is assuaged through Solnit's tie to landscape rather than bloodlines.

Solnit constructs comparisons between the United States and Ireland in order to further illustrate the theory of bioregionalism as a type of landscape acculturation. To this end, Solnit's narrator definitively declares that:

> American conversations tend to be dialectical, a give and take of short statements, or even more laconic, the kind of monosyllabic exchanges so popular in tough-guy texts and television. In the West and even more in the Western, silence is a sign of strength. Ireland has a different conversational economy, one in which the ability to talk well is a gift and perhaps even a weapon, for the political disenfranchisement and powerlessness of the Irish people and the Irish language under an English government are often described as silence. (45)

Solnit's definitive descriptions of national conversational styles are then linked, once again, directly back to bioregionalism. "Someone," she informs readers, "once suggested to me that styles of speech resemble the landscapes they emerge from, that one can trace the flatness of the plains in raw midwestern accents, desert silence in western taciturnity, the lushness of the southeast in its denizens' dulcet tones" (45). Solnit thus manages to elide conceptions of identity as tied to bloodlines while still preserving essentialist notions of identity that address the problems of assimilation. It is more than merely ephemeral culture which constructs us, it is also the landscape that shapes and feeds our commonality. Solnit then goes on to argue that "[t]he same could be said of Ireland, whose intricate, winding landscape is so densely and intricately scored with the stones and wounds of history, and whose musically rising and falling speech can hardly proceed without anecdote" (45). We are, literally, home grown by the very earth upon which we walk. Solnit re-legitimizes conceptions of national identity by re-territorializing its springs.

The contradictions contained in Solnit's narrative reveal a turbulent maelstrom of anxieties about the legitimacy of national identity. Solnit's discourse of discomfort troubles essentialist notions of national identity. On the other hand, Solnit's determination to proffer a universal solution to anxieties surrounding national identity within the demands of globalization, and her desire to cling to essentialist notions of identity as evidenced in her sentimentalized construction of Ireland, make opaque the depth and breadth of the centripetal and centrifugal forces currently shaping contemporary social reality on a global scale. Solnit's inability to move outside the epistemological space provided by modernism, in spite of her deliberate attempts to do so through her engagement with the discourse of discomfort, exposes one of the vexed borders of contemporary identity politics as the United States attempts to re-imagine itself in a global era.

Notes

[1] Other identity theorists, such as Arjun Appadurai in *Modernity at Large: Cultural Dimensions of Globalization*, would argue that we are already moving to a form of postnational or transnational identity. Solnit's text helps to expose the tensions between these two positions.
[2] Although I would argue that declaring one does not intend to work within genre conventions, as a means of announcing one's ethical awareness, now almost seems to be emerging as a convention itself.
[3] The term "globalization" can be used in many ways. Here, I refer to the imagination of the earth as a single, living planetary system on which all members are ethically responsible for its continued well-being.
[4] The Project on Globalization, Identity Politics, and Social Conflict, "an international collaborative research project" claims that "the relationships between socio-political and economic phenomena such as globalization, identity-politics and different forms of social conflict are usually most concretely, immediately and effectively encountered and expressed in social-cultural discourse and texts in the public domain" (http://www.open.ac.uk/Arts/gipsc/noframes/index.html). I would argue that travel narratives, because of their configuration of Self and Other and their expectations surrounding their truth-value, uniquely fulfill these criteria.
[5] This awareness can appear more obliquely than it does in Solnit's narrative, as when Paul Theroux anticipates critique of his representations by somewhat testily declaring his subjectivity in *Pillars of Hercules: A Grand Tour of the Mediterranean* (1995). Theroux admonishes readers who might question his perceptions with, "That was your trip, that was your Italy. This book is about my trip, my Italy. This is my Mediterranean" (7). Several years later, in his added postscript to *Dark Star Safari* (2003/04), Theroux, less-testily, remarks:

> The journey ends, the traveler goes home, the book gets written. The result, the travel narrative, implies that it has fixed the place forever. But that is a meaningless conceit, for time passes, the written-about place keeps changing. All you do as a note-taking traveler is nail down your own vagrant mood on a particular trip. The traveling writer can do no more than approximate a country. (473)

[6] The extensive works Solnit references in her notes include Dean MacCannell's interview on tourist and military complexes in *Headland Journal* (1994), Edward Said's *Culture and Imperialism* (1993), Elaine Scarry's *The Body in Pain: The Making and Unmaking of the World* (1985), Derek Walcott's "The Muse of History" (1995), Michael Ignatieff's *Blood and Belonging: A Journey into the New Nationalism* (1994), Simon

Schama's *Landscape and Memory* (1995), and George Santayana's "The Philosophy of Travel" (1994).

[7] In this sense, I combine Benedict Anderson's concept of the role imagination plays in building communities with Arjun Appadurai's concept of the construction of postnational imagery in *Modernity at Large*.

[8] As Smith remarks in *National Identity*, nationalism "provides the sole vision and rationale of political solidarity today, one that commands popular assent and elicits popular enthusiasm" and that "[a]ll other visions, all other rationales, appear wan and shadowy by comparison. They offer no sense of election, no unique history, no special destiny. These are the promises which nationalism for the most part fulfils, and the real reasons why so many people continue to identify with the nation" (176-77). Smith also argues that it is nationalism's ability to "provide a satisfying answer to the problem of personal oblivion" which makes it so powerful, and that "[i]dentification with the 'nation' in a secular era is the surest way to surmount the finality of death and ensure a measure of personal immortality" (160). While both of these arguments are important to consider, they do not fully explain the types of stresses surrounding identity revealed by Solnit's narrative.

[9] In "Images of Irish Americans," Susan Dente Ross argues, to the contrary, that stereotypical images of Irish Americans are so ubiquitous they are virtually invisible (132).

[10] See Noel Ignatiev's *How the Irish Became White* for a markedly different interpretation of this process.

[11] I use the phrase "modernist longing" here in order to emphasize with the epistemological basis of deeply felt emotional states.

[12] Assimilation is obviously still highly valued in the United States, but multiculturalism, as an alternative, is now more highly valued than previously.

Works Cited

Anderson, Benedict. *Imagined Communities*. Rev. ed. London: Verso, 1991.

Appadurai, Arjun. *Modernity at Large: Cultural Dimensions of Globalization*. Minneapolis: U Minnesota P, 1996.

Dezell, Maureen. *Irish America: Coming into Clover*. New York: Doubleday, 2001.

Fabian, Johannes. *Time and the Other: How Anthropology Makes its Object*. New York: Columbia UP, 1983.

Ignatieff, Michael. *Blood and Belonging: A Journey into the New Nationalism*. New York: Farrar, Straus, and Giroux, 1994.

Ignatiev, Noel. *How the Irish Became White*. New York: Routledge, 1995.

Kenny, Kevin. *The American Irish: A History*. New York: Pearson Education, 2000.

MacCannell, Dean. *Headlands Journal*. Sausalito, CA: Headlands Center for the Arts, 1994.

—. *The Tourist: A New Theory of the Leisure Class*. Berkeley: U California P, 1976.

O'Connor, Barbara. "Myths and Mirrors: Tourist Images and National Identity." *Tourism and Ireland: A Critical Analysis*. Eds. Barbara O'Connor and Michael Cronin. Cork: Cork UP, 1993. 68-85.

Project on Globalization, Identity Politics, and Social Conflict. Ed. Suman Gupta. 17. Dec. 2002. The Open University, UK. 20 May 2005. <http://www.open.ac.uk/Arts/gipsc/noframes/index.html>.

Ross, Susan Dente. "Images of Irish Americans: Invisible, Inebriated, or Irascible." *Images that Injure: Pictorial Stereotypes in the Media*. Eds. Paul Martin Lester and Susan Dente Ross. 2nd ed. Westport, CT: Praeger, 2003. 132-38.

Said, Edward. *Culture and Imperialism*. New York: Knopf, 1993.

Santayana, George. "The Philosophy of Travel." *Altogether Elsewhere: Writers on Exile.* Ed. Mark Robinson. New York: Harcourt, 1994.

Scarry, Elaine. *The Body in Pain: The Making and Unmaking of the World*. New York: Oxford UP, 1985.

Schama, Simon. *Landscape and Memory*. New York: Knopf, 1995.

Smith, Anthony D. *National Identity*. Reno: U Nevada P, 1991.

Solnit, Rebecca. *A Book of Migrations: Some Passages in Ireland.* London: Verso, 1997.

Theroux, Paul. *Dark Star Safari*. Boston: Houghton Mifflin, 2003/04.

—. *The Pillars of Hercules: A Grand Tour of the Mediterranean*. New York: G. P. Putnam's Sons, 1995.

Walcott, Derek. "The Muse of History." *Post-Colonial Studies Reader*. Ed. Bill Ashcroft, Gareth Griffiths, and Helen Tiffin. London: Routledge, 1995.

CHAPTER THREE

THE SOURCE, THE MOVIE, AND THE REMAKE: IMPERIAL NOSTALGIA IN ISAK DINESEN'S *OUT OF AFRICA*, SYDNEY POLLACK'S *OUT OF AFRICA*, AND MELINDA ATWOOD'S *JAMBO, MAMA*

JEANNE DUBINO

I had a farm in Africa [. . .]
—*Out of Africa* 3

I announced that there was nothing to worry about because "I had a fah-rm in Ah-frica," doing my impression of Meryl Streep doing her impression of Karen Blixen.[1]
—Atwood 2

Redolent of the past, the opening line from Isak Dinesen's *Out of Africa* is the most famous from the book, not because of its popularity as a text but because of its popularization in Sydney Pollack's movie version.[2] Beginning with this line, the lavish, Oscar award-winning movie version of *Out of Africa* continues to inform many Americans' impressions of Kenya,[3] including Melinda Atwood's, who, in her travel book *Jambo, Mama*, self-admittedly echoes Meryl Streep's accent and phonetically highlights two key words in both hers and Dinesen's books: *farm* and *Africa*. Like Dinesen, Melinda Atwood spent a long stretch of time in Kenya—six years to Dinesen's seventeen. Like Dinesen, whose coffee plantation was the basis of her world, Atwood made her house the center of her life in Kenya. And, like Dinesen, Atwood sought to establish an enterprise in Kenya—cottage industries to Dinesen's coffee plantation—only to leave. Several years upon their return in their home countries, Denmark and the United States, they published their first books: Dinesen, *Out of Africa* in 1937 (before that, *Seven Gothic Tales* in 1934) and Atwood, *Jambo, Mama* in 2000. Dinesen went on, as we know, to become a renowned author, while Atwood resumed her career as a professional dancer, choreographer, and producer.

Atwood's book is a testimony to the power that movies can wield in shaping our conception and attitude toward the past. Atwood freely acknowledges the role that Pollack's *Out of Africa* played in her decision to go to Kenya and in the life she set up for herself while she was there:

> I had spent the months before heading to Africa pouring over books on Kenya, to say nothing of wearing out my copy of the videotape of 'Out of Africa.' Not only had I memorized all the best dialogue and had Meryl Streep's accent down pat, I had also fashioned a very romantic image of my future life in Kenya [. . .] I wanted atmosphere, history, and the air of foreign intrigue. (18)

Atwood declares here that she wants to recreate the "quaint and colonial" (18) life portrayed in the movie *Out of Africa*, one of "atmosphere, history," and "intrigue." In preparing for this romantic life, Atwood tells us that she did not wear out the copy of the book *Out of Africa* but, rather, her copy of its movie version.

It is worth examining how the single-book author Atwood, with her eye on Pollack's movie, follows in the footsteps of the far more illustrious Dinesen. Generically different—Dinesen's *Out of Africa* is a pastoral memoir (Langbaum 135), Pollack's is a Hollywood nostalgia film, and *Jambo, Mama* is a light autobiography and travel book—all offer a nostalgic view of colonial Kenya. Written retrospectively, from the vantage point of the Western home countries of Denmark and the United States, *Out of Africa* and *Jambo, Mama* are reminiscences of a past life spent in a foreign country that is itself perceived by the West as the past. Considered to be one of the backward regions of the world, sub-Saharan Africa continues to be a location defined by its relation to the developed regions of the globe in terms of its distance in space and in time. Africa's constructed remoteness in space and time draws many first-world travelers, like Dinesen and Atwood, to it. This paper first complicates the kinds of nostalgia that motivate their travels: while Dinesen's takes on a reflective quality, Atwood's is one marked by an active quest to restore the past. "The Source, the Movie, and the Remake" next addresses the role that popular film plays in influencing contemporary travelers' perceptions of the past: not only do sixty-three years separate the two works, but so does a movie that, even now, continues to shape Westerners' impressions of Africa. Finally, this chapter explores the ways that a representative colonial settler like Dinesen and a representative contemporary privileged traveler like Atwood remember the past, respectively, in the discourses of the pastoral and anecdotal, the timeless and topical, and the serious and comical.

In its most literal meaning, nostalgia means a longing for home and, in its etymological roots, for one's homeland. Though its origins are from ancient Greek, it was first coined in late seventeenth-century Switzerland, as Svetlana

Boym writes in *The Future of Nostalgia*, as a term to define a disease suffered by "various displaced people of the seventeenth century, freedom-loving students from the Republic of Berne studying in Basel, domestic help and servants working in France and Germany and Swiss soldiers fighting abroad" (3): namely, an ache for one's home country. Over the centuries, however, the yearning for home has increasingly been replaced by a yearning for the past. Parallel to this shift in the object of loss from the spatial to the temporal is a changing conception of time. Until the full onset of modernity, as David Lowenthal writes, "men scarcely differentiated past from present, referring even to remote events, if at all, as though they were then occurring" (xvi). "For many millennia," he continues, "most people lived under much the same circumstances as their forebears, were little aware of historical change, and scarcely differentiated past from present" (xvi). Now that we are aware of change, now that we know that change separates us from what was and what we were, we develop a sense of loss and longing. Nostalgia, thus,

> is a yearning for a different time—the time of our childhood, the slower rhythms of our dreams. In a broader sense, nostalgia is rebellion against the modern idea of time, the time of history and progress. The nostalgic desires to obliterate history and turn it into private or collective mythology, to revisit time like space, refusing to surrender to the irreversibility of time that plagues the human condition. (Boym xv)

With this consciousness, the history of literature itself comes to be defined by nostalgia, as Raymond Williams brilliantly writes in *The Country and the City*.[4] British literature tends to be the literature of loss.[5] Williams calls this consciousness of loss a "crisis of perspective" (35); for Williams, Western, especially British, pastoral poets underwent continuing crises in their restless search for a pastoral ideal, for a golden age, "a pre-capitalist and therefore irrecoverable world, [. . .] the safer world of the past" (36). Williams writes, "When we moved back in time, consistently directed to an earlier and happier rural England, we could find no place, no period, in which we could seriously rest" (35). The pastoral poetry of each era, as Williams shows, is marked by unhappiness with the present state of instability and by a longing for the supposed order of the era preceding it, an order located in the country. Thus it is that "the common image of the country is now an image of the past" (Williams 297) and, concomitantly, "an idea of the country is an idea of childhood" (Williams 297). (The city, in contrast, becomes the "image of the future" [Williams 297].)

With the contemporary era, the "model of city and country, in economic and political relationships, has gone beyond the boundaries of the nation-state and has become the model of the world" (Williams 279) or the "system we now know as imperialism" (Williams 279). From having been associated with the country, the past is now displaced onto the underdeveloped countries. Like Williams's, David Lowenthal's language also captures the identification of the past with the other and with the exotic, an identification, I will add, that began with the rise of British imperialism: "Only in the late eighteenth century," Lowenthal writes in *The Past is a Foreign Country*, "did Europeans begin to conceive the past as a different realm, not just another country but a congeries of foreign lands endowed with unique histories and personalities" (xvi). What is notable here is the association of the past not only with foreign places but also with the very process of imperialism: Lowenthal draws an extension from a different realm to another country to "a congeries of foreign lands" (xvi). It is hardly to be wondered that nostalgia has taken on the additional and slightly pejorative connotation of an idealization and romanticization of the past.

If writers attempt to realize their nostalgic desire to return to the past through the imagination, the rest of us may realize ours, as Dean MacCannell writes in his groundbreaking book *The Tourist*, through travel. MacCannell describes how contemporary travel is propelled by an anaclitic yearning for the past: "For moderns, reality and authenticity are thought to be elsewhere: in other historical periods and other cultures, in purer, simpler lifestyles" (3). Where Williams focuses on the restlessness of pastoral poets for a happier past marked by tranquility and calm, MacCannell addresses moderns' quest for the authentic. Moderns travel elsewhere in their search for reality—a reality found in the nonmodern world (MacCannell 8). Caren Kaplan adds, "When the past is displaced, often to another location, the modern subject must travel to it, as it were [. . .] Displacement, then, mediates the paradoxical relationship between time and space in modernity" (35).

Renato Rosaldo addresses the political significance of this yearning for "other historical periods and other cultures" with his concept of imperial nostalgia. Imperial nostalgia is a self-explanatory term—a longing for an earlier era—that masks, Rosaldo writes, a more sinister agenda: imperial nostalgia "uses a pose of 'innocent yearning' both to capture people's imaginations and to conceal its complicity with often brutal domination" (70). Imperial nostalgia is not just, as Ian Baucom would add, "an allegorical historiography of loss and redemption. These imperatives of redemption and return are not [. . .] simply local to the domestic discourses of Englishness; they also structure the practices of empire" (271). In tracing the progression from the "innocent yearning" in the book *Out of Africa* to its film version to the travel book *Jambo, Mama*, we see an ever attenuating hold on a colonial vision, which is then transformed into an idealized and unrealizable dream. *Jambo, Mama* is demonstration of what Rojek and Urry call "the performativity of reminiscence" (14), a process that encrusts "the original object with secondary images" (14) values, and associations, in turn making us "lose sight of the original meaning of the object" (14) and engaging our "complicity with often brutal domination" (Rosaldo 70). The original meaning, then, becomes "co-opted to fulfill temporary, immediate personal or cultural interpretations" (Rojek, "Indexing" 59). This paper addresses primarily the "original" source of *Jambo, Mama*—that is, the book version of *Out of Africa*—and the ways Atwood co-opts Dinesen to fulfill her own temporary and immediate personal or cultural interpretations, with reference to how this co-optation is "encrusted" with images and references to the movie.

As a nostalgic film, Pollack's *Out of Africa* plays a significant intervening role between Atwood and her original source. With its romanticized representation of the past, the "nostalgia film" is not properly historical but, rather, is a "desperate attempt to appropriate a missing past [. . .] now refracted through the iron law of fashion change" (Jameson 18). Frederic Jameson further emphasizes "that the nostalgia film was never a matter of some old-fashioned 'representation' of historical content, but instead approached the 'past' through stylistic connotation, conveying 'pastness' by the glossy qualities of the image, and '1930s-ness' or '1950s-ness' by the attributes of fashion" (19). The narrower category of "colonial nostalgia film," such as *Out of Africa,* recreates the colonial past with the same attention to sartorial detail and setting as a Ralph Lauren advertisement series.

The general transmogrification of movies into stylistic and glossy advertising enables the idealization of the past that informs nostalgia film. Mark Crispin Miller describes the way movies increasingly tend "to look and sound a lot like TV commercials, as if the major film schools were teaching not, say, the best movies out of Warner Brothers but the latest campaign by the Saatchi brothers. Like ads, movies now tend to have a perfectly coordinated total look, as if they'd been designed rather than directed" (49). Crispin Miller describes how the "ad technique" of "idealizing and disjointed images" or "pseudo-narrative" (57) has "drastically reduced the movies' narrative potential" and turned it, at the very least, "into a poundingly hypnotic instrument—a mere *stimulus*" (50). In movies, now, story is transformed into "spectacle" (Crispin Miller 64) or "daydream" (Crispin Miller 57).

The bulk of Crispin Miller's article addresses the way movies, featuring name-brand products, have increasingly become vehicles for advertisements, and, as Lowenthal writes, for the past itself. Movies have helped to alter our perception of the past. Returning to the roots of nostalgia, we are reminded that a longing for the past is not only a longing for other historical periods and other cultures, but also for the familiar, the comfortable—that is, for home. When we visit the past, as Lowenthal notes, we tend to domesticate it, to make its strangeness familiar and homelike. Movies enable us to fetishize the past and to "bring it into the present as a marketable commodity" (Lowenthal xxv).

With movies, the very character of recollection is transformed (Lowenthal xxii). Because movies tend not to maximize content but rather to focus on fast-paced editing, as Svetlana Boym wryly notes, "attention deficit disorder indeed might become a cure for old-fashioned longing that took too much time for daydreaming and thinking" (39). Movies tend to eschew the mournful; with their happy endings, they offer, as Crispin Miller writes, "the same reassurance, at once authoritarian and easygoing, that we discern in advertising" (67):

> Abrupt, illogical, unmotivated, the new happy ending is, as narrative, a total washout. And that is precisely what it's meant to be: each cheery climax functions not to end the story but to liquefy it. As everybody seems to melt into the spectacle, the "problems" that had kept the story going, however minimally, need no longer be resolved, because this sweetest of all pleasures has *dissolved* them—in the bliss of being in the spectacle. (Crispin Miller 67)

Indeed, continues Crispin Miller, movies do not exactly promise a happy ending but, rather, no ending. They "conclude their 'narratives' without seeming to terminate them, as if to assure us that the spectacle will never end at all" (67). They prefer the dazzling if not impossible conclusion of a "techno-fairy tale" (Boym 33) over the sad resolution of a "mournful elegy" (Boym 33).

With their rapid-fire editing, their easy conclusion (or alternately, their promise of no ending), their slick and stylistic ahistorical representation of history, and their attempt to appropriate the past for its use for the present, movies, and more particularly nostalgia films, fall into the category of what Boym would call "restorative nostalgia" (41). Restorative nostalgia "manifests itself in total reconstructions of monuments of the past" (41). The restorative nostalgic seeks to return to "the original stasis, to the prelapsarian moment. The past for the restorative nostalgic is a value for the present; the past is not a duration but a perfect snapshot. Moreover, the past is not supposed to reveal any signs of decay; it has to be freshly painted in its 'original image' and remain eternally young" (Boym 49). Throughout *The Future of Nostalgia,* Boym contrasts restorative nostalgia with an opposing category: reflective nostalgia. Where restorative nostalgia focuses on the return to home, the reconstruction of home, the relevance of home to the present, reflective nostalgia, writes Boym, "thrives in *algia*, the longing itself, and delays the homecoming—wistfully, ironically, desperately" (xviii). It "dwells on the ambivalences of human longing and belonging" (xviii); it "lingers on ruins, the patina of time and history, in the dreams of another place and another time" (41).

Applying Boym's dichotomous definition of nostalgia to *Out of Africa* and *Jambo, Mama*, we can see that, while both books share a longing for the past and while both figure the past as Kenya and in Kenya, the nature of that longing differs. Where *Out of Africa* is reflective, *Jambo, Mama* is more restorative. In *Out of Africa*, the past becomes the pastoral. Dinesen's quest for a pastoral past is furthermore represented as a kind of Wordsworthian love affair with nature in all its attendant poignancy.[6] Dinesen's ache is prolonged and deep, dwelling on a timeless and irrecoverable world. The quality of Atwood's representation, on the other hand, is as fast moving and as episodic as a television program. Informed by the contemporary media, and abounding with references to it, the more anecdotal *Jambo, Mama* breezes over the very descriptions, particularly of the landscape and animals, over which Dinesen lingers. So light and topical is *Jambo, Mama* that one might even dismiss it from serious consideration. Yet, it is worth examining, both in its role as an heir to its more serious predecessor and, perhaps more importantly, as a response to the Hollywood version of *Out of Africa*.

In the style of the pastoral, Isak Dinesen lavishes attention on the landscape. Her first five words—"I had a farm in Africa"—set the tone for the book to follow. As Lewis points out, this opening sentence "establishes her having (or having had) the farm as the point of departure for the whole book, without any history of prior possession, without any reference to negotiation or purchase" (2), and without, he adds, the murder and destruction that colonial takeover generally involves, as it certainly did in Kenya.[7] Writing about colonial landscapes, David Bunn notes that:

> any form of temporal reference—even geologic time, the time of erosion and sedimentation—is potentially threatening because it may remind of prior historical violence that prepared the way for this foreign invasion. Time, in other words, is experienced in a peculiar way. The settler landscape cannot afford the Romantic luxury of bathing in the past, in deep history, because the past is the domain of the Other, and history is the history of dispossession. (143)

The bird's-eye view offered at the beginning of *Out of Africa* further allows the onlooker to distance herself spatially from the details of the quotidian present and to imagine in their place a timeless, romantic and heroic otherworld filled with scenes of "full rigged ships with their sails clewed up" (*Out of Africa* 3).[8] Focusing on the ethereal quality of the air, Dinesen distills a sense of timelessness out of the geographical position of the farm:

> The height of the land combined to create a landscape that had not its like in all the world. There was no fat on it and no luxuriance anywhere; it was Africa distilled up through six thousand feet, like the strong and refined essence of a continent [. . .] The chief feature of the landscape, and of your life in it, was the air. Looking back on a sojourn in the African highlands, you are struck by your feeling of having lived for a time up in the air [. . .] Up in this high air you

> breathed easily, drawing in a vital assurance and lightness of heart. (*Out of Africa* 3-4)

For Dinesen, a view from the skies is even grander than observing the plantation from a hilltop; she describes flying in a plane "the most transporting pleasure in [her] life" (*Out of Africa* 237) because of the view it affords:

> above the African highlands, surprising combinations and changes of light and colouring, the rainbow on the green sunlit land, the gigantic upright clouds and big wild black storms, all swing around you in a race and a dance. The lashing hard showers of rain whiten the air askance. The language is short of words for the experiences of flying, and will have to invent new words with time. When you have flown over the Rift Valley and the volcanoes of Suswa and Longonot, you have travelled far and have been to the lands on the other side of the moon. You may at other times fly low enough to see the animals on the plains and to feel towards them as God did when he had just created them, and before he commissioned Adam to give them names. (238)

Dinesen is hardly short of words here; like the Old Testament God creating, from on high, the world below, she generates, from her lofty vantage point, a scene of words. Hers is a painterly view, with its swaths of color and kinetic perspective, with its Dionysian dance of clouds and rain. As beautiful as this word-painting is, we cannot forget that landscape is not merely a "genre of painting or fine art" but is, rather, "best understood as a medium of cultural expression" (Mitchell 14). Landscape mediates between nature and culture, and as such has a semiotic structure, like money (Mitchell 15). In this passage, the sense of expansion, of traveling as far as "lands on the other side of the moon," is suggestive of "the discourse of imperialism" conceived as an "expansion of landscape," inevitable and natural (Mitchell 17). At the same time that Dinesen conveys a sense of the sublime—a sense that words cannot describe what she has seen—she also adopts, as she had in the preceding passage, a godlike and imperial persona, with the power to see and to name and to possess an entire land, one all the more transcendent for its absence of people.[9] But even when indigenous Kenyans are present, they are naturalized as part of the landscape, "Africa in flesh and blood":

> The Natives are in accordance with [the landscape], and when the tall, slim, dark, and dark-eyed people travel,—always one by one, so that even the great Native veins of traffic are narrow foot-paths, or work the soil, or herd their cattle, or hold their big dances, or tell you a tale, it is Africa wandering, dancing and entertaining you. (*Out of Africa* 21)

In the spirit of the pastoral, Dinesen transforms the harsh realities of plantation labor. It is at its most picturesque when the faces of the laborers indistinguishably blur into the darkness of the night and adorn it, much "like a bright jewel in an Ethiope's ear" (*Out of Africa* 8). Her house servant Kamante is also described in painterly and picturesque language, hardly a human, more a fantastic gargoyle: "A fantastic figure he always was, half of fun and half of diabolism; with a very slight alteration, he might have sat and stared down, on the top of the Cathedral of Notre Dame in Paris" (*Out of Africa* 32).

Animals, on the other hand, are personified, particularly her deerhounds (one of whom has a "noble profile" [*Out of Africa* 70]) and, above all, Lulu, a gazelle she has adopted, the embodiment of a precious kind of femininity. Lulu has:

> large quiet purple eyes. She had such delicate legs that you feared they would not bear being folded up and unfolded again, as she lay down and rose up. Her ears were smooth as silk and exceedingly expressive. Her nose was as black as a truffle. Her diminutive hoofs gave her all the air of a young Chinese lady of the old school, with laced feet. It was a rare experience to hold such a perfect thing in your hands [. . .] She was extraordinarily neat in all her habits. She was headstrong already as a child [and alternately] a young wife who pertly permits her husband a caress, [. . .] a real shameless young coquette. (*Out of Africa* 68, 71)

For Dinesen, "[t]he years in which Lulu and her *people* [emphasis added] came round to my house were the happiest of my life in Africa" (*Out of Africa* 78). This detailed and humanized portrait of a gazelle stands in contrast to the relatively homogenized characterization of the Kenyans with whom Dinesen lives.

In its overwhelming attention to the natural beauty of the setting, to its flora and fauna (including its representation of Africans as fauna), *Out of Africa*, true to its genre as a pastoral, excludes current events. Dinesen eschews references to contemporary politics; we do not know who was in power from reading *Out of Africa*. We see few of the real-life occurrences and incidents that are attendant on running a large farm or, more accurately, plantation. Dinesen compresses "eighteen years of drought, mismanagement, and struggle, the endless petty quarrels with the shareholders and intrigues with bankers, the terrible fluctuations of international coffee prices, and the vagaries of the weather" (Thurman 282) into: "it was hard work to keep it going" (*Out of Africa* 7).

The eighteen years that Dinesen was in Kenya, from 1914-1931, witnessed the Great War, the influenza pandemic, the beginning of the Great Depression, and, more relevant to the White Highlands, the massive displacement of Kikuyu and Masai from their land.[10] Yet, only incidental mention is made of this background. The society Dinesen describes of her fellow-aristocrats "is a static, even anachronistic thing; it is not white-settler culture (which she largely scorns), but the culture of an earlier age and distant place" (Lewis 65). In his article "Culture, Cultivation, and Colonialism in *Out of Africa* and Beyond," Simon Lewis goes on to analyze *Out of Africa* "in terms of the European tradition of pastoral" (63). Lewis's analysis also addresses the "timeless authenticity" of the Masai (65), the re-presentation of aristocrats wearing the courtly masks of shepherds and indulging in an Arcadian existence (66), Dinesen's care for her workers (66), and, finally, the bemoaning of the passing of the feudal order, "of which she and Finch Hatton (sic) were exemplars" (71).[11]

Finch-Hatton's death at the end *Out of Africa* consummates the loss that characterizes the book, beginning from the first line of the novel—"I *had* a farm in Africa" (3, emphasis added). It caps the elegiac tone for a world well lost even before the memoir began. Dinesen describes Finch-Hatton's death in fatalistic terms, as something inevitable, as the loss of an ideal and the end of an era: "For many years after this day the Colony felt Denys's death as a loss which could not be recovered. Something fine then came out in the average colonist's attitude toward him, a reverence for values outside their understanding" (351). Dinesen does not just mourn the loss of her farm and her soul-mate; she also laments the days when "all Africa was a real deer-park" (70). No longer, however; "now it was slowly changing and turning into a business proposition" (223). Dinesen does not indicate an awareness that it is settlers like herself who are responsible for this transformation.[12] What Mitchell says about landscape in a postcolonial and postmodern era is true for the colonial era as well: "[l]ike imperialism itself, landscape is an object of nostalgia in a postcolonial and postmodern era, reflecting a time when metropolitan cultures could imagine their destiny in an unbounded 'prospect' of endless appropriation and conquest" (Mitchell 20). Returning to Rosaldo's definition of imperial nostalgia, we are reminded that it revolves "around a paradox: A person kills somebody, and then mourns the victim. In more attenuated form, somebody deliberately alters a form of life, and then regrets that things have not remained as they were prior to the intervention" (Rosaldo 69).

Out of Africa exudes timelessness not just through its genre as a pastoral but also as a tale. In her biography *Isak Dinesen: The Life of a Storyteller*, Judith Thurman writes that "*Out of Africa* is the 'story' of Isak Dinesen's life told according to her own rigorous laws of storytelling and faithful to her own understanding of what a tale is and must be" (285).[13] While tale, of course, can be broadly defined, as a general term describing a simple narrative (Harmon and Holman 512-13), it is often a shorthand version of folktale, associated with timelessness and placelessness, like the pastoral, as something outside history, "not bounded by one continent or one civilization" (Thompson 5). Carole Martin Shaw explains how the very structure of Dinesen's tale creates a "sense of time out of time" (193). The book is not divided into chapters but into five major sections, the longest of which is divided into thirty-two subsections, or little stories, and the shortest of which is divided into four subsections. Shaw writes that the "resulting fragmentation denies the reader anticipation, creates no internal tension; neither chronology nor character is consistently developed. Hard times come and go, people join the household and grow older, others pass through, even wars happen, [but] all change is on the surface—Africa is essentially timeless" (Shaw 192-93).

Africa is not essentially timeless in *Jambo, Mama*. Although Atwood makes a passing mention of the "reality" of "timelessness" in her suburb—"Nothing changed at the Karen Dukas [stores]. Year after year, it was always the same" (Atwood 49)—the reality of her book reminds us of the changing present. *Jambo, Mama* is topical. It may be motivated by a desire to recreate the allure of the past, but its references sweep its readers along the present day. In addition to the echoes of the movie *Out of Africa*, the brief mention of events, the uses of slang, allusions to contemporary and popular culture, photographs, references to products and corporations, all serve to remind readers of its historical specificity. The stock market crash of October 1987 (65) marks the approximate beginning of Atwood's sojourn and the "escalating war in the Gulf" (284) ends it. We have "wannabe" (56), Jane Fonda work-out tapes (45), comparisons to Mel Gibson (5) and the Three Stooges (9), references to *The Jeffersons* (286), *The Cosby Show* (286), *New York, New York* (13), *Gone with the Wind* (21), photographs indicating the fashions of the late 1980s and early 1990s, Kellogg's Corn Flakes (52), and AT&T (54).

With its topicality, *Jambo, Mama* is an anti-pastoral. Atwood does attend to the beauty of the land around her in fleeting moments, such as her first view of the Ngong hills from her first house, but she quickly delivers her description in the pat image of a "180-degree postcard view" (23). This spirit-lifting vision of "the Africa [she] had been dreaming about" (23) is welcoming to her not for the beauty that inheres in it but because it distracts her from her disappointment over the gaudiness of her rental home. Far from the "little 'settler's cottage'" (23) she had envisioned for herself, her new home is cavernous and gloomy, its rooms done up in "all brown" (22) or "Kelly green" (22) or "cathouse pink" (23). The attention she pays to the 1970s tacky décor outweighs the delight she takes in the landscape.

In its concern about the ugly realities of dated interior decoration, *Jambo, Mama* works[14] against the pastoral ideal. Rather than the describing the rosy-fingered dawn that appears every morning in equatorial Africa, Atwood paints a humorous picture of her pink bedroom:

> It was a symphony in pink and gold. Everything was covered either in pink silk or pink velvet or trimmed with pink fringe. The dressing table was white with gold flowers, but it did have a pink velvet stool. The bedspread and drapes pulled the whole scheme together: they were pink and gold cut velvet. (22)

But with the view of the Ngong Hills from her patio, she damns her "pretentious house" with all its "endless velvet." If, she writes, "I could just sit on this patio and look at the Ngongs and smell the air in Africa, I just might live through the year I had signed on for. I would just never go downstairs again. Or I would redecorate. I suddenly didn't care" (23). In the manner of a picaresque tale, the rest of *Jambo, Mama* recounts Atwood's determined efforts to make a life for herself in Kenya.

In place of Dinesen's stylized sketches and tales, recounted randomly and nonsequentially, Atwood's anecdotes carry us forward and chronologically from the search for her first house to the sale of her second. Chapter by chapter, Atwood narrates the predicaments in which she finds herself as she moves from a life of leisure, dotted by safaris, to her entrepreneurial projects as the owner of cottage industries. Along the way she recounts incidents in the life of her household, her interactions with her visiting friends and the local expatriates, and her not-so-grand love affair. Where Dinesen favors the far-off and otherworldly, Atwood hones in on the anti-romantic quotidian and on her immediate surroundings, including, for example, the condition of the roads to her suburb Karen: "Driving a car in Kenya is about as close as you can come, without actually pointing a loaded revolver at your head, to playing Russian Roulette" (Atwood 47). The next five paragraphs provide a gritty description of Kenyan roads: populated with farm animals wandering about, they are pocketed with pot holes which fill with water during the rainy seasons and may be further booby-trapped with nails by would-be criminals and thieves at night. True to her character, however, Atwood tells us, "I eventually became so cool headed that I could avoid the pot holes, swerve around any goats, and down shift with my left hand while I groped for a lipstick behind the passenger seat" (48).

Whether from the United States to Kenya, or within Kenya itself, Atwood's ease of mobility was made possible by her class position: like Dinesen, Atwood was independently wealthy (Atwood xiv). While Dinesen never expresses any unease with her class position—indeed, she wears her title of Baroness proudly—Atwood does express some discomfort over her wealth (194), as a result of which she lives on a smaller scale than she otherwise could have. As a first-worlder, however, Atwood, like her colonial predecessor, takes for granted her unobstructed passage through her environment (Bunn 135). "When I was in Africa," she writes, "I was comfortable in ways I had never been comfortable before: comfortable in my skin, comfortable in my clothes, and comfortable with myself. I was happy, and maybe for the first time in my life, at peace" (25).

This comfort, and the concomitant freedom of movement, as David Bunn writes about the colonial settlers in early nineteenth-century South Africa, "is the ultimate indication of being at home in an environment; having free passage and moving, according to whim, with a naturalness like the passage of breezes or rivers also masks the artificiality of the colonial presence" (139). Their privilege not only allows them to roam freely in a land populated with people whose lives are constricted by the rigors of labor; it also allows them to escape the confinement that is still the lot of the majority of women's lives.[15]

Yet, paradoxically, what matters most to each woman when she arrives in Africa is setting up house, the ultimate symbol of confinement. No sooner does each arrive than she sets out to reproduce the very institution that she leaves, and those institutions take on, furthermore, the same symbolic value. Is setting up home the cure for nostalgia? For Dinesen, at any rate, the house would additionally be "an oasis of civilization" (Thurman 108). The word "oasis" stands out here; in fact, in the colonial landscape, the house became a site of "ideological dissemination," a point "from which [. . .] standards of taste and civility radiate out into loneliness" (Bunn 150). What Ian Baucom writes about the significance of the country house in England applies as well to the country house in its colonies:

> The country house [. . .] ramifies beyond its own domestic space; it is resonant with more than merely local significance. It signifies both Englishness and empire, the manifestation in England's built space of colonial capital and colonial discipline. It represents an authorized and elite—but increasingly hegemonic—order of English belonging which is not only financed by the acts of colonial possession, but which finds in the disciplinary protocols of colonial administration a model for its own procedures of identity formation and reformation. (261)

The colonial house not only signifies English imperialism and is financed by it, but it also functions to help build the metropole, the "house of modern British capitalism" (Baucom 263). While generally the colonial estate in Kenya was modeled on the plantocracy of the American South (Elkins 10), for Isak Dinesen the estate was based on capital, as Lewis writes, rather than land. She farmed only a thousand of out the 6,000 acres for coffee on behalf of the Karen Coffee Company. Though, in private, her letters are filled with references to her home and to her farm, in her published memoir, as Lewis notes, her "interest in the farm is secondary to interest in the park" (70). He adds, "[w]hile Dinesen does relatively little as a farmer in the memoirs, her hunting experiences provide occasion for some of the most detailed and intense descriptions in the books. She uses them to show herself in an almost elemental relationship with an Africa, which in turn makes her and her hunting partner (Finch-Hatton) into almost mythic figures outside whose 'torchlight there was nothing but darkness'" (70).

While *Jambo, Mama* lacks the dreamy and nostalgic atmosphere of its published and cinematographic predecessors, it is nostalgic nevertheless in its recounting of Atwood's quest to rebuild Dinesen's home—specifically, the home as it is featured in the movie. Pollack's *Out of Africa* was released in the same decade as other films celebrating the British empire, including *The Jewel in the Crown*, *Gandhi*, and *A Passage to India*, all "fantas[ies] of return to the pleasures of the imperial past" (Baucom 261). These "imaginative return[s] to the glories of imperial dominance" (Baucom 261) are not unrelated to Atwood's desire to recreate a "settler cottage." In her dreams of Africa, Atwood channels longing and desire into house-hunting and remodeling. She fantasizes not the landscape, the Kenyan people, or even what she would do, but the house she would live in: "I wanted to live in [. . .] Karen Blixen's [house] [. . .] The house I was to live in was a major player in my fantasy life that summer" (Atwood 18). Dinesen's house was also the center for the lush and expansive cinematography in Pollack's film; in her dream of Africa, Atwood seeks to recreate the movie setting, which itself attempts to restore the "prelapsarian moment," to cite Boym again. Atwood buys a dilapidated house literally located in Karen, a suburb of Nairobi, and situated on the former site of Dinesen's estate.[16] She meticulously furnishes her replication house, even down to the details of bringing her mother's old clock (Atwood 270), reminiscent of Dinesen's cuckoo clock (*Out of Africa* 46), which also figures in the movie. At least four chapters of *Jambo, Mama* are devoted to the year Atwood spent searching for and remodeling her house, and she includes as well a number of before and after photos.

The past does indeed figure in *Jambo, Mama* as a "perfect snapshot"; looking like pictures from *Better Homes and Gardens*, the after-photos indeed reveal an "eternally young" past. The photos also recapture one of the great American myths, the theme of the make-over. The greatest pain Atwood feels on departing Kenya is the fear that her house, the house that she spent months restoring, will be torn down: "It was painful for me to sell that house at all, but wondering whether someone was just going to just tear it all down and graze their cattle on the land almost broke my heart" (311; as it turns out, her house was not torn down). For Dinesen, estate means capital; for Atwood, it means the dwelling itself. Both of these definitions stand in contrast to Kenyans' conceptions of property, which are intrinsic to the land itself, as Atwood informs the reader:

> The low value placed on a property's actual dwelling stems from the old Kenyan ways of doing things. Temporary houses, or more likely mud huts, were not what

> gave a property its value. Fertile land which could be used to grow crops, raise cattle and divide up among your offspring, did. (311)

Both Dinesen and Atwood sought to make a home in Kenya, but that was not their only reason for moving there. The kind of nostalgia that motivated their quests is not limited solely to setting up a dwelling away from one's home country. As we have seen, nostalgia, when applied to the privileged traveler, encompasses a wider range of motives, including the quest for roots, sources. For first-world travelers like Dinesen and Atwood, the real, the authentic, is found in Marlow's "blank spaces on the earth" (Conrad 9) or in the underdeveloped countries of the world. So too, as for Marlow, is the opportunity for adventure and for freedom to feel themselves at home—particularly, for women, freedom to realize themselves in a manner denied them in their home countries.[17] Both Dinesen and Atwood traveled out of a general sense of adventure (Thurman 106-07), but Dinesen's was an adventure she shared with her husband, Bror, whom she accompanied as his wife. There would have been little other opportunity otherwise for a woman of her time to see "the great world," something she wanted to do ever since she was a young girl (Thurman 41).

Melinda Atwood first went to Kenya in 1985 for a short jaunt, just after she saw *Out of Africa*. This first visit planted the seed for a desire to return, a desire intensified, as she candidly admits on the first page of her Prologue, by another motive: to run away from her family, and out of a fear of becoming just like her mother (xiii), "who, after four husbands had come and gone, would still accept nothing but the opinion of some man as a reflection of her worth" (xiv). Having married and divorced twice by the time she was twenty seven, Atwood was well on her way toward fulfilling her mother's destiny. Running away and embarking on a "grand adventure" (xiii) gave her the opportunity to escape it.

Unlike Atwood, Dinesen does not baldly state her motives in her memoir. In fact, she does not reveal her motives at all. They are beside the point. For all that *Out of Africa* is a memoir, Dinesen reveals little about her personal life. She does not typically refer to her marriage or divorce; to her affair with Denys Finch-Hatton (who figures in the memoir as a friend and, at the end, as a soul-mate); nor to her syphilis. She does not turn herself into a feminist hero. Instead, she creates a persona for herself that fits in with the pastoral quality of *Out of Africa*. Dinesen does not show herself to be a stranger in a strange land, nor does she show the process that it takes for her to become accustomed to her new home. Rather, from as early as the second page of her memoir, she represents herself as of a piece with the landscape: "In the highlands you woke up in the morning and thought: Here I am, where I ought to be" (*Out of Africa* 4).

Among the Africans, she places herself magnificently at the center of her new world: "The discovery of the dark races was to me a magnificent enlargement of all my world" (*Out of Africa* 17). Playing all roles, she is herself a figure of plenitude; to "her" Africans, she is a doctor (23, 24), a judge (104), a priest (86), a guardian angel (271), and, predictably, the white man—in this case, white woman—carrying the white man's burden: "It is a heavy burden to carry a farm on you. My Natives, and my white people even, left me to dread and worry on their behalf, and it sometimes seemed to me that the farm-oxen and the coffee-trees themselves, were doing the same. It appeared to be agreed upon, then, by the speaking creatures and the dumb, that it was my fault that the rains were late and the nights so cold" (323). To the Africans, she is not only the legendary fisherman's wife who seeks to control the weather, she is, as a white, the weather itself: Africans "inflict upon you a role not of your own choosing, as if you were a phenomenon in Nature, as if you were the weather" (127). She has the aura of a symbol (a "brass serpent" [106]) and, even more, of a god itself. She imagines that, if the Africans "like or esteem you at all, it is in the manner in which people love God; not for what you do to them, not at all for what you do to them, but for what you are" (128; *cf.* 374). Without her, this pastoral world she has created is incomplete; just before she leaves Kenya, she imagines that "[i]t may have been to them difficult, and daring, to imagine the world without me in it, as if Providence had been known to be abdicating" (385).

As Carole Martin Shaw sardonically notes, while colonialists such as Dinesen "saw themselves as gods," the Kikuyu whom she interviewed "imagined the colonialists as bringing disease" (11). Clearly, in envisioning themselves as gods, the colonialists did not indicate, to use litotes, a high degree of self-awareness. However, again, that was not Dinesen's purpose for *Out of Africa*; she intended to write a pastoral. Robert Langbaum, one of her champion critics, more vigorously states her motives in the following passage:

> Isak Dinesen has been able to reinvigorate the romantic tradition because she rediscovered in Africa the validity of all the romantic myths, myths that locate spirit in the elemental—in nature, in the life of primitive people, in instinct and passion, in aristocratic, feudal, and tribal societies that have their roots in nature. She could not, however, have seen Africa as she did had she not brought to it eyes prepared by European romanticism, had she not discovered Europe in Africa. (119)

Atwood, on the other hand, in performing Streep performing Dinesen, conveys in *Jambo, Mama* a fairly high degree of self-awareness which subverts the authority of the colonial mask, however idealized that mask may be. Here it is useful to pause to consider the practice of performativity. As Linda Hutcheon writes, performance can be regarded as a forward and positive postmodern activity, "one that uses and abuses, installs and then subverts, the very concepts it challenges" (1), that "asserts and then deliberately undermines such principles as value, order, meaning, control, and identity" (13). Performance triggered by nostalgic reminiscing may not necessarily imply a conservative yearning for the past but, rather, in postmodern fashion, becomes a "critical revisiting, an ironic dialogue with the past" (Hutcheon 4). Such critical revisiting can be perceived as "challenging and questioning" (Hutcheon 8). Certainly, *Jambo, Mama* bears out Atwood's desire to fashion "a very romantic image of [her] future life in Kenya" (Atwood 18), even if she later mocks herself playing this role on several occasions, when, for example, she is sick: "'You fancy yourself Karen Blixen. Or Margaret Mead. You are the Great White Huntress! No? Did those women fall apart with a few minor inconveniences? A runny tummy? I should say not'" (129).

It is more likely, however, that such challenging and questioning is itself a form of co-optation, in line with what Mary Louise Pratt theorizes in her study *Imperial Eyes* as an "anti-conquest" narrative (38-68).[18] This concept resembles imperial nostalgia in that it uses innocence as a guise. Writes Pratt, "the conspicuous innocence" of the traveler (Pratt here refers specifically to nineteenth-century naturalists) "acquires meaning in relation to an assumed guilt of conquest, a guilt the naturalist eternally tries to escape, and eternally invokes, if only to distance himself from it once again" (57). Having witnessed the ugly, harsh realities of the "contact zone," the discourse of nineteenth-century travelers "turns on a great longing: for a way of taking possession without subjugation and violence" (Pratt 57). In response to Pratt, Fowler writes that the "act of conquest ('invasion') produces guilt that the narrator 'eternally tries to escape' and yet 'eternally evokes, if only to distance himself from it once again'" (210).

The following passage from *Jambo, Mama* offers a telling take on Pratt's notion of the anti-conquest:

> Ever since I was a teenager, I had wanted to have one "Grand Adventure." At one point in my life, I had thought that spending a year abroad, in Rome or Paris perhaps, would have been exciting. But with the discovery of Africa, that idea had paled considerably. Every safari in Kenya surpasses the one before it, and with each 'personal best,' my desire for the next thrill rose ever higher. And I couldn't get high enough. Until the NFD. [Northern Frontier District, officially renamed the North Eastern District after Independence (Atwood 105)]. Then there we were, the Great White Hunter and I, in the middle of the adventure of a lifetime, like being dropped into a movie. Granted, they didn't call "cut" at the end of each scene, and I was not helicoptered back to my air-conditioned Winnebago in time for dinner. But that made it more exciting. This was "real" and quite unbelievable. All the more so because I was the one who was doing it. (129)

At first Atwood seems to ironize her grand adventure by placing it in quotation marks. Her grand adventure, she seems to suggest, will pale next to those that took place before her. She seems to be referring to the clichéd trope of discovery, and we might anticipate her attempting to break free from this trope, so "instrumental in the construction of rationales for imperialism" (Kaplan 53). But no; we read that the thrill of traveling in Western Europe is not as great as the thrill of traveling in Africa. She does not seek to outdo others but, rather, her own earlier accomplishments. Her life centers on achieving her "personal best" or, more precisely, on a succession of thrills. In the middle of the passage, her language breaks down, and she writes in fragments. We then read that what makes traveling to the North Eastern District exciting for her is not the thought of danger (and the North Eastern District is off-limits to all but the most hardy and determined tourists), but, rather, the thought of feeling like she is in a movie (recall Boym's "techno-fairy tale" [33]). She is not mocking herself here, as she had in her earlier passage; she is expressing genuine delight. Her innocence of the adventurers who preceded her and her position in relation to them, as a neo-adventurer with the means to travel about on a whim, bespeak a certain frivolity, if not a measure of self-centeredness and lack of awareness of her role as a rich white Western woman traveling in a country whose per capita income is less than a dollar a day—that is, a contact zone.[19]

Like other directors who have made movies in Kenya,[20] Pollack could have hardly failed to see the contact zones of Kenya, he altogether ignores them in his movie. He also ignores Dinesen's self-representation in his representation of her life. The great allure of Pollack's *Out of Africa* is not the representation of Dinesen as a brave and independent, if imperious and arrogant, woman managing a large plantation on her own. Rather, it is the portrayal of her relationship with Denys Finch-Hatton. The first person Dinesen meets in the film is Denys, though, in real life, Dinesen did not meet him until several years after her move to Africa (Cooper and Descutner 242). Cooper and Descutner further note that the "key phrase in the opening monologue that sets the tone for the film is: 'He was waiting for me there' [. . .] Africa, too, was waiting for her, but the continent and its people pale in comparison with Finch Hatton (sic); men, not Africa, will be the focus of the film" (Cooper and Descutner 242). Indeed, the grand, Hollywood-style love affair portrayed by Meryl Streep and Robert Redford is the focus of the film. Crispin Miller's point that Hollywood elevates "stardom over narrative" (58) is borne out here. It is the celebrity culture that made Pollack choose Redford as the leading man and that made Redford refuse to take on an English accent in his role as Finch-Hatton—he preferred to play himself. It is also the celebrity culture that has drawn so many people to the Karen Blixen Museum located in her old house. Since the release of the film in 1985, the crowds have doubled, and there is hardly a web site for the Museum that does not capitalize on the movie (see, for example, Meacham) and few that do not warn browsers that "Denys Finch-Hatton was no Robert Redford" (Morgan).

From the first line of her book, Dinesen sets the focus on herself and on Africa. Though in real life she may have been married and divorced to one man and in love with another, we would not know that from reading *Out of Africa*. Atwood, on the other hand, admits immediately to having been married and divorced twice by the time she was twenty seven and does recount, in some detail, her love affair in Kenya, inspired, she candidly admits, by the film. The main draw for the "settler's cottage" she buys is her imagined picture of "Denys Finch-Hatton sitting on the back veranda" (165). Perhaps she really meant Robert Redford playing Denys Finch-Hatton. She does, indeed, find her Redford as Finch-Hatton in the figure of the bush pilot Simon West, the next best thing to a Great White Hunter (82). But West is as unavailable to her as Finch-Hatton was to Dinesen.

It is worthwhile here to consider the three versions of Finch-Hatton—as he appears in the movie, the memoir, and in life. In both the movie version and the life story, commitment, for Finch-Hatton, was equivalent to fetters. The movie suggests that Finch-Hatton was a philanderer; the biography indicates that he was both a philanderer and bisexual (Shaw 195). The philandering and possibly bisexual real Finch-Hatton does not appear in the book version of *Out of Africa*. Instead, Dinesen makes, in the fictionalized version of Finch-Hatton, a companionable character for her fictionalized self-representation. That is, in the memoir, Dinesen, looking back with nostalgia, creates a relationship based on equality between herself and her lover. Interestingly, Atwood, on the other hand, does not idealize her relationship or herself in the relationship. Unlike the figure of independence that Dinesen creates in her memoir, Atwood portrays herself as gullible and lovesick, falling for a man known among her circles as "'The Most Dangerous Animal in the Mara'" (81). But, unlike Dinesen, Atwood does not keep the myth of her great white hunter substitute alive; she acknowledges, at the end of her memoir, that "right from the start, [. . .] this man cheated on [her] and lied to [her]" (283). By the end of her memoir, Atwood has deconstructed her earlier romantic yearnings.

Dinesen represents herself as singularly solitary on her estate, reminiscent of Andrew Marvell's unaccompanied speaker in his arch-pastoral poem "The Garden."[21] Dinesen sets herself apart from the people with whom she lives, whether those people are her servants, her neighbors, or her soul-mate. Lewis notes that:

> what is interesting is precisely the inclusion of reified groups of peasantry, laborers, and "natives" at the expense of the boring bourgeoisie: farm managers, accountants, agents, and the like. *Out of Africa* gives the impression that Karen

> Blixen had unmediated connection with her work force, that the day-to-day running of the farm depended on her personality as a kind of primum mobile. (66-67)

Dinesen rarely includes dialogue; few voices are heard, and even more rarely do we hear those of the Kenyans among whom she lives. Even Dinesen's defenders admit that she is "guilty of taking away their voices" (Cooper and Descutner 231). Dinesen may have acted as doctor, teacher, and nursemaid to her staff, but, true to the requirements of the pastoral, these "honorable actions toward the Kenyans can be attributed more to a sense of *noblesse oblige* than to any assumed equality" (Cooper and Descutner 230). She consistently refers to the people who work in her house in the possessive—*e.g.,* "my house-boys" (341). "Even Blixen's care for 'her' laborers and squatters, elevating her role within the agricultural community against less scrupulous neighbors, puts *Out of Africa* in the same category as Ben Jonson's *To Penshurst* in which the so-called 'moral economy' prevails," writes Lewis, and then, citing Raymond Williams, he adds, "Blixen's memoirs present the farm, exactly as *To Penshurst* does, as the site of a 'natural order of responsibility and neighbourliness and charity'" (Lewis 66). When she must leave, she feels, true to her sense of *noblesse oblige*, the greatest concern over those whom she allowed to squat on her land (*Out of Africa* 373, 378). What does appease her is her success in securing a piece of territory in the Kikuyu Reserve for all of the two families and their cattle (Thurman 249).[22]

Just as Atwood spends more time describing her romantic involvement, so does she elaborate in more detail than Dinesen on her relationships with her extensive household staff and the workers in her cottage carpet and needlepoint industries. Devoting chapters to each of the three main house workers in her life in Kenya, Atwood looks closely after her housekeeper Mildred when she falls ill (249), spends time with Lucy through her death (197-215), and attends to Celestine when she has her baby (216-33). Like Dinesen, who nurses her beloved "houseboy" Kamante to health, Atwood is maternal toward her employees. Unlike Dinesen, Atwood makes genuine attempts to forge relationships based on genuine equality, most notably, with Mildred. In spite of having "been told repeatedly to follow the very strict dictates concerning the dealings with one's staff," Atwood "tossed that rule out straight away" (36), beginning with Mildred. Atwood writes,

> We certainly did not have any background in common, although we did have sons the same age; but we seemed to understand each other. I appreciated her warmth and the fact that she seemed to be looking out for me. I, in turn, took care of her. She also had the enormous good sense to laugh at my jokes, or at least smile at all the right places. Mildred was the first person I saw every morning and

> the last one at night, and I came to be honestly fond of her. I felt she liked me as well, or at least I hoped so. (36)

Atwood's recognition that Mildred *seemed* to understand her, *seemed* to look out for her, "smile[d] at all the right places," and may *not* have fully reciprocated in her affection toward her, indicate her respectful attempt to see from her house-worker's point of view. Additionally, early on in her memoir, Atwood recognizes that the lack of jobs may make her employees so eager to please her, but, little versed in global demographics, she attributes this lack to overpopulation, when in fact Africa's population density was the same as the United States. Too, she un-ironically concludes here, like any good late Victorian, that "finding good help" is so hard these days (30). Nonetheless, respectful of the ways of the country, she insists, "I was trying to do things as they were done in [Kenya]" (194-95). In *Jambo, Mama*, Atwood recounts many of the scenes (*e.g.,* 112-13) and, more significantly, replays many of the dialogues that she has with her household and factory workers. This replay of dialogue is significant, because it demonstrates an attempt to give Kenyans a voice. Moreover, Atwood freely acknowledges her workers' vagaries, such as her house-worker Daniel's cleaning out her safe of all its foreign currency (35). While Dinesen may mark tribal differences among the Kenyans, she still romanticizes them as an inscrutable Other, if an other whom she ranks above her fellow English expatriates (Cooper and Descutner 234). Atwood, on the other hand, distinguishes among the Kenyans with whom she works and admits when she fails to do so, such as her inability to recognize a driver of a vehicle from its more important passenger and their "tribal differences as well" (41).

Of course, it cannot be denied that, in publishing *Jambo, Mama,* Atwood capitalizes on the stories of her life among the Kenyans, just as Dinesen has in *Out of Africa*.[23] Moreover, like Dinesen, Atwood benefits from their labor. Atwood also takes advantage of the Karen Blixen/Isak Dinesen legend. She appeals to travelers' nostalgic imperialism in the choice of her business—specialty, non-assembly-line carpets featuring "primitive animal designs" (Atwood 171), a design surely confirming an aesthetic preconception of Africa as a primitive continent—and in the choice of its locale. Writes Atwood, "We might be able to encourage the tourists to come by after their requisite visit to the Karen Blixen Museum" (167).

After seventeen years, Dinesen left Kenya because she could not make her coffee plantation pay; the soil was too acidic, and the rainfall insufficient (Thurman 107). Just as her arrival fits in with the pastoral tradition, so does her departure. As Lewis writes, Dinesen:

> shows a marginal interest in conserving the farm, the farm animals, and the old country ways, but extracts the existence of farm laborers. Playing a variation on

> that theme in *Out of Africa,* Karen Blixen shows a marginal interest in conserving Kenya, its animals, and native ways; however, any pleas she makes on behalf of her farm laborers are muted by her equation of them with wildlife, possessions, or the land itself. (75)

Furthermore, he notes, even if it wasn't her intention, her work lends "itself to further commercialization by a culture that has long been involved in the selling of the continent—its people, its land, its natural resources" (Lewis 75).

After six years, Atwood left for a variety of reasons: her failed relationship with the ne'er-do-well Simon West, her homesickness for the United States, her constant hassles of running a business with forty employees, and her loneliness. In spite of her attempts to set up house, to plant roots, she never was really accepted into the expatriate community: "When I bought my little house, I was sure that would make things feel more settled and indicate to everyone that I was there to stay. I hoped that would make me more socially acceptable. But it didn't" (301). Atwood's quest to make a home in Kenya, to feel at home in Kenya, failed. What most triggered her departure, however, was the increasing rate of crime—the car-jackings (304) and her beloved house being broken into. Atwood's nostalgic vision of a "'Fahrm in Ah-frica'" (29) was destroyed by her experience with the urban violence, the "endless bribery and endemic corruption" (Atwood 304) that accompany imperialism. Atwood does not seem to realize that her country's fabulous state of wealth is based, in part, on first-world policies that allow if not encourage the kind of third-world corruption that eventually drives her out.

Unlike their squatters and employees, Dinesen and Atwood have the freedom to leave when they are not able to realize their dreams of a life in Africa. Having attempted to recreate the mystique of the lives of past generations, they return home. Their dream of an imperial life in Africa is transformed to a nostalgic dream of Africa.

Notes

[1] Both *Jambo, Mama* and Pollack's movie version of *Out of Africa* refer to Isak Dinesen by her official name Karen Blixen, as do a number of the authors whom I cite. Throughout my article I will consistently refer to Dinesen by her pen name.

[2] "If ever Oscars were awarded for famous lines spoken in outrageous accents, then the all-time winner should probably be Meryl Streep for her opening words in *Out of Africa.* Remember them? 'I had a faarrm in Aff-reek-kaa, at the foot of the Nee-gong hills'" (Meacham).

[3] See Meacham, and also Gacheri.

[4] See also Baucom 271.

[5] Boym notes that mass culture also arose at the same time that nostalgia "as a historical emotion came of age" (16).

[6] Compare also Pico Iyer, who writes,

> For if every true love affair can feel like a journey to a foreign country, where you can't quite speak the language, and you don't know where you're going, and you're pulled ever deeper into the inviting darkness, every trip to a foreign country can be a love affair, where you're left puzzling over who you are and whom you've fallen in love with. All the great travel books are love stories, by some reckoning—from the Odyssey and the Aeneid to the Divine Comedy and the New Testament—and all good trips are, like love, about being carried out of yourself and deposited in the midst of terror and wonder. (Iyer, "Why We Travel")

[7] For two of the latest histories of British rule in Kenya, see Caroline Elkins's *Imperial Reckoning* and David Anderson's *Histories of the Hanged.*

[8] See Shaw 181.

[9] On the painterly vision, see Wolfson. On the absent landscape, see Gurnah.

[10] For the Kikuyu and Masai displacement, see especially Anderson and Elkins.

[11] Denys Finch-Hatton's name is commonly hyphenated; however, Lewis and Cooper and Descutner choose not to use the hyphen.

[12] Shaw also notes the way that colonialists, having claimed "the wilds of Africa as their happy hunting ground" (181), ended up "slaughtering many of the species Western environmentalists now try to protect" (181).

[13] Dinesen prided herself as a teller of tales, as a storyteller, a "member of an 'ancient, idle, wild and useless tribe,' with her roots in the oral tradition and her power from a charged complicity with those who listened" (Thurman 348).

[14] In considering Atwood's despair over the décor of her new house, one is reminded of Oscar Wilde, who is reported to have said, near the very end of his life, "'My wallpaper and I are fighting a duel to the death. One or the other of us has to go'" (Ellmann 581).

[15] See Frye 82.

[16] Interestingly, it is popularly thought that Karen is named after Blixen herself, but it is not; rather, it is named after Blixen's cousin Karen Melchior, "whose father was the chairman of the Karen Coffee Company Ltd." (Trillo 163).

[17] Compare, again, Iyer, who writes, "When, some years ago, my family home suddenly burned to the ground in a forest fire, and all my photos, mementos and notes were reduced to ash, I was reminded forcibly again that home nowadays has nothing to do with a piece of soil and everything to do with something I carry around inside me" (Iyer, "The Journey Home").

[18] John Gruesser writes about the way contemporary travel literature,

> particularly when it involves someone from the West writing about someplace in Africa, has become increasingly problematic. In one sense, the unapologetically imperialistic late-nineteenth- and early-twentieth-century travel writing about Africa was much more honest than either the escapist *entre les guerres* accounts which often quietly urged a more benign colonial system or the anti-colonial books that began to appear in the days before widespread independence and have continued into the postcolonial era [. . .] As the postcolonial era in Africa enters

its fourth decade, can Western writers continue to write the same old travel book—with the map in the front, an account of the journey into the interior, perhaps an epiphany or two along the way, and a summary statement contrasting Africa and the West? (361)

[19] To be fair, elsewhere in her travel book Atwood does indicate that she is fully aware of the meager pay of the Kenyans with whom she lives, and she does pay the people who work in her house and in her factories an above-average wage (*e.g.*, 290).
[20] After rhapsodizing over the beauty of the landscape, Caroline Link, whose nostalgia film *Nowhere in Africa* is also set in Kenya, described Kenya as a land of "incredibly ugly cities, dilapidated villages, unspeakable poverty" (Link).
[21] "Such was that happy garden-state, / While man there walked without a mate" (1700).
[22] Cooper and Descutner note that "[i]n Dinesen's accounts, other European settlers, unlike herself, neglected their aristocratic obligations by failing to protect and provide for the less privileged" (232).
[23] At the same time, it must be noted that the impetus for writing a published book did not come from Atwood herself. From the very first page, in her Acknowledgments, she declares, "I never dreamed of writing this book. It was not my idea to start with, and left on my own, I never would have started it, finished it, or ever seen it in print. I owe all that to others" (v). Though it is a trope of travel writing to disavow one's desire to publish one's narrative, Atwood's account of the eight-year writing history of *Jambo, Mama* is detailed enough to sound convincing.

Works Cited

Anderson, David. *Histories of the Hanged: The Dirty War in Kenya and the End of Empire*. New York: W. W. Norton, 2005.
Atwood, Melinda. *Jambo, Mama*. Ft. Bragg, CA: Cypress House, 2000.
Baucom, Ian. "Mournful Histories: Narratives of Postimperial Melancholy." *Modern Fiction Studies* 42.2 (1996): 259-88.
Boym, Svetlana. *The Future of Nostalgia*. New York: Perseus, 2001.
Bunn, David. "'Our Wattled Cot': Mercantile and Domestic Space in Thomas Pringle's African Landscapes." *Landscape and Power*. Ed. W. J. T. Mitchell. Chicago: U of Chicago P, 2002. 127-73.
Conrad, Joseph. *Heart of Darkness*. 1899. New York: Pocket Books, 1972.
Cooper, Brenda, and David Descutner. "'It Had No Voice to It': Sydney Pollack's Film Translation of Isak Dinesen's *Out of Africa*." *Quarterly Journal of Speech* 82.3 (1996): 228-50.
Dinesen, Isak. *Out of Africa*. 1937. New York: Random House, 1965.
—. *Seven Gothic Tales*. New York: H. Smith and R. Haas, 1934.
Elkins, Caroline. *Imperial Reckoning: The Untold Story of Britain's Gulag in Kenya*. New York: Holt, 2005.
Ellmann, Richard. *Oscar Wilde*. New York: Knopf, 1988.

Fowler, Corinne. "The Problem of Narrative Authority: Catherine Oddie and Kate Karko." *Gender, Genre, and Identity in Women's Travel Writing*. Ed. Kristi Siegel. New York: Peter Lang, 2004. 209-24.

Frye, Marilyn. "Oppression." *Women's Voices, Feminist Visions: Classic and Contemporary Readings*. Ed. Susan M. Shaw and Janet Lee. 2nd ed. Boston: McGraw-Hill, 2004. 80-82.

Gacheri, Jayne Rose. "The Karen Blixen Coffee Garden That is Immortalised." *Life Magazine – Sunday Standard* 27 Apr. 2003: 14.

Gruesser, John C. "Nostalgia Incarnate." Rev. of *The Black Heart: A Voyage into Central Africa*, by Paul Hyland. *African American Review* 26.2 (1992): 361-63.

Gurnah, Abdulrazak. "Settler Writing in Kenya: 'Nomenclature is an Uncertain Science in these Wild Parts.'" *Modernism and Empire*. Ed. Howard J. Booth and Nigel Rigby. Manchester, UK: Manchester UP, 2000. 275-91.

Harmon, William, and C. Hugh Holman. *A Handbook to Literature*. 7th ed. Upper Saddle River, NJ: Prentice-Hall, 1996.

Hutcheon, Linda. *A Poetics of Postmodernism: History, Theory, Fiction*. New York: Routledge, 1988.

Iyer, Pico. "The Journey Home." *Time Online*. 11 Aug. 2003. 15 Oct. 2005 <http://www.time.com/time/asia/ 2003/journey/story.html>.

—. "Why We Travel." *Salon.com*. 18 Mar. 2000. 15 Oct. 2005. <http://archive.salon.com/travel/feature/2000/03/18/why/print.html>.

Jameson, Frederic. *Postmodernism, or, The Cultural Logic of Late Capitalism*. Durham, NC: Duke UP, 1991.

Kaplan, Caren. *Questions of Travel: Postmodern Discourses of Displacement*. Durham, NC: Duke UP, 2000.

Langbaum, Robert. *The Gayety of Vision: Isak Dinesen's Art*. New York: Random House, 1965.

Lewis, Simon. "Culture, Cultivation, and Colonialism in *Out of Africa* and Beyond." *Research in African Literatures* 31.1 (2000): 63-79.

Link, Caroline. "Voluptuous Landscapes, Incredibly Ugly Cities." *The East African* 24-30 Mar. 2003: II.

Lowenthal, David. *The Past Is a Foreign Country*. Cambridge: Cambridge UP, 1985.

MacCannell, Dean. *The Tourist: A New Theory of the Leisure Class*. 1976. Berkeley: U of California P, 1999.

Marvell, Andrew. "The Garden." *The Norton Anthology of English Literature*. Ed. M. H. Abrams. 7th ed. Vol. 1. New York: W. W. Norton, 2000. 1698-1700.

Meacham, Steve. "Ghosts of Africa." *Sydney Morning Herald Online* 12 Feb. 2005. 15 Oct. 2005 <http://www.theage.com.au/news/Africa/Ghosts-of-Africa /2005/02/11/1108061863200.html?oneclick=true#top>.

Miller, Mark Crispin. "Hollywood the Ad." *Atlantic Monthly* April 1990: 41-68.

Mitchell, W. J. T. "Imperial Landscape." *Landscape and Power*. Ed. W. J. T. Mitchell. 2nd ed. Chicago: U of Chicago P, 2002. 5-34.

—. Introduction. *Landscape and Power*. Ed. W. J. T. Mitchell. 2nd ed. Chicago: U of Chicago P, 2002. 1-4.

Morgan, Judith. "A Visit to the Karen Blixen Museum, Nairobi." *Copley News Service* 1998. 15 Oct. 2005 <http://www.karenblixen.com/visit.html>.

Pollack, Sydney, dir. and prod. *Out of Africa.* Perf. Robert Redford and Meryl Streep. Videocassette. MCA Home Video, 1986.

Pratt, Mary Louise. *Imperial Eyes: Travel Writing and Transculturation.* London: Routledge, 1992.

Rojek, Chris. "Indexing, Dragging and the Social Construction of Tourist Sights." *Touring Cultures: Transformations of Travel and Theory*. Ed. Chris Rojek and John Urry. London: Routledge, 1997. 52-74.

Rojek, Chris, and John Urry. "Transformations of Travel and Theory." *Touring Cultures: Transformations of Travel and Theory*. Ed. Chris Rojek and John Urry. London: Routledge, 1997. 1-19.

Rosaldo, Renato. *Culture and Truth: The Remaking of Social Analysis*. Boston: Beacon, 1989.

Shaw, Carolyn Martin. *Colonial Inscriptions: Race, Sex, and Class in Kenya.* Minneapolis: U of Minnesota P, 1995.

Thompson, Stith. *The Folktale*. 1946. Berkeley: U of California P, 1977.

Thurman, Judith. *Isak Dinesen: The Life of a Storyteller*. New York: St. Martin's, 1982.

Trillo, Richard. *The Rough Guide to Kenya*. 7th ed. N.P. 2002.

Williams, Raymond. *The Country and the City*. New York: Oxford UP, 1973.

Wolfson, Leah. "Biography." 1998. 15 Oct. 2005. <http://www.english.emory.edu/Bahri/Blixen.html>.

CHAPTER FOUR

FIREBRAND AND THE CAT: THE IMPOSSIBILITY OF CLOSURE AND WILLIAM BYRD'S HISTORIES OF THE DIVIDING LINE

RUSS POTTLE

In an analysis of autobiography, Paul DeMan argues that "the interest of autobiography [. . .] is not that it reveals reliable self-knowledge–it does not–but that it demonstrates in a striking way the impossibility of closure and of totalization (that is the impossibility of coming into being) of all textual systems made up of tropological substitutions" ("Autobiography" 922). DeMan's conclusions about the impossibility of closure in autobiography can be translated to travel writing through examining the companion narratives *History of the Dividing Line betwixt Virginia and North Carolina* and *The Secret History of the Line* by William Byrd of Westover, the English gentleman who lived between London and the royal colony of Virginia in the seventeeth and eighteenth centuries. The relationship between these two narratives, which describe from differing perspectives a foray along the boundary dividing Virginia from the charter colony of North Carolina, enlivens the relationship between travel writing and autobiography and presents a fascinating opportunity to employ critical and scholarly writing about autobiography in exploring the contours of travel literature.

Confronting Phillipe LeJeune's assertion that autobiography "is not only representational and cognitive but contractual, grounded in speech acts," DeMan argues that autobiography is instead a series of displaced and substituted tropes, a "whirlygig" of figures within a text (922-23). Borrowing from Gérard Genette the metaphor of a child's toy that spins at a breath of air, always a blur of motion between presence and absence, DeMan illustrates that autobiography is at once the giving and the taking away of its subject, a process of face and defacement. This motion between the positive and the privative, the truthful and the untruthful, and the impossibility of separating them, brings autobiography in critical proximity to travel literature. It casts light on the relationship between Byrd's histories, even as it signals a connection between autobiography and travel writing and provides perhaps a figure or metaphor though which theoretical discussions of travel literature might be advanced.

Byrd and the Two Histories

Byrd's histories were begun in 1728, when the wealthy Virginia landowner helped to lead two parties of surveyors to re-mark the boundary between North Carolina and Virginia. The original line had been set from the location of an end or inlet to the Currituck River. Over time, this geographical feature had become less distinctive, either in response to the inevitable change in course of rivers or because the names of some elements surrounding it had changed, and location of the line had become the subject of controversy. To settle the question, each colony provided a number of "commissioners" to oversee the work of surveyors, who were to mark the line from its origin to what Byrd calls a location "within the Shadow of the Chariky Mountains [. . .] at least Six Hundred Miles" inland (318-320). The number of commissioners and surveyors, plus logistical support, amounted to probably a total party of fifty (Smith 300).

The expedition generated a great deal of paper, mostly in the form of surveyors' reports and maps. Byrd himself logged personal notes of the journey in a shorthand developed by the writing master William Mason (Anderson 709-710). A number of Byrd scholars have rolled Byrd's note-taking during the survey into his famous project of diary writing, but Richard Beatty Croome, a Byrd biographer, and Jeffrey Folks argue that Byrd may have begun the notes as a method of validating expense accounts (Croome 135-36; Folks 4). Whatever their genesis, the notes eventually were worked by Byrd into two separate, though closely related, narratives of the survey party's travel through the towns and villages and, finally, the swamps and wilds that lay along the colonies' dividing line.

In some ways, the narratives look much alike. They follow the same chronological structure, and from time to time Byrd went so far as to copy verbatim passages from one into the other. In some ways, however, the narratives look very different. One account, which we will call the *History*, was most likely intended for publication, either among Byrd's circle of natural science colleagues or among a larger reading public. As Louis B. Wright, Byrd's editor for Harvard University Press, explains, Byrd had been elected to the Royal Society in 1696, at the age of twenty-two, and had presented to the Society a paper on albinism the next year (7). A life-long interest in natural phenomena, combined with membership in the Royal Society and his experiences in the untamed Virginia landscape, probably accounted for Byrd's interest in writing the *History*. According to Wright and others, Byrd's class anxiety probably accounted for his not publishing the *History* further than in manuscript. Wright reports that in 1737 Byrd was seeking illustrations for his text, an indication that serious publication may have been in the cards, but for unknown reasons he abandoned the endeavor. A victim as well as a member of the gentle classes, Byrd may have been uncomfortable with being perceived as merely a writer (Wright 1-2; Berland, et al. 36-37; Siebert 535-36).

The text that came from this aborted effort is indeed the sort of hybrid that falls under the terms "travel narrative" or "travel writing." Part natural history, part ethnography, part scientific report, couched in the narrative structure of a journey to there and back, and clearly involved in the Western imperial project, the *History* reflects both the more "literary" characteristics ascribed to eighteenth-century travel writing and the more "realistic," power-centered discourse that would be constructed in nineteenth-century travel writing (Alami, par. 1; Russell 2). The eighteenth-century values are apparent in allusions to literary texts of travel, such as Chaucer's *Canterbury Tales* (Anderson 711) or the more contemporary *Robinson Crusoe* (Byrd 72); to biblical texts that speak to both Old and New Testaments (Anderson 721-22); in the "instructive" or didactic purpose that informed the literature of Byrd's time (Anderson 712; Russell 4); and in the detatched style that was common to gentlemen's writing in that period (Berland et al. 36-37; Siebert 541). These latter attributes appear in, for instance, Byrd's regular comments about the poor physical condition of North Carolinians, whose reliance on pork as a dietary staple had put them in what Byrd considered to be quite a fix:

> The only Business here is raising of Hogs, which is manag'd with the least Trouble, and affords the Diet they are most fond of. The Truth of it is the Inhabitants of N. Carolina devour so much Swine's flesh, that it fills them full of gross Humours. For want too of a constant Supply of Salt, they are commonly obliged to eat it Fresh, and that begets the highest taint of Scurvy. Thus, whenever a Severe Cold happens to Constitutions thus Vitiated, tis apt to improve into the Yaws, [. . .] and lastly shews its spite to the poor Nose, of which tis apt in a small time treacherously to undermine the Foundation.
>
> This Calamity is so common and familiar here, that it ceases to be a Scandal, and in the disputes that happen about Beauty, the Noses have in some Companies much ado to carry it. (54)

In this passage, Byrd unites both moral instruction and style, commenting on the wages of indolence he perceives among his neighbors to the south and employing a satirical tone to emphasize his own urbane presence in the narrative. Yet the text also shows the beginnings of the realist, empire-centered style of the nineteenth century. Byrd could be maddeningly elliptical in his personal diaries (Anderson 702-707), but the *History* seeks to record nearly everything that crossed Byrd's path or that resonated in his experience and store of knowledge. For instance, Byrd's use for medicinal purposes of sap from the sweet-gum tree includes a comparison of that commodity to ambergris, which itself engenders a discussion of the production and uses of ambergris, "in Order to reconcile the various Opinions concerning it" (278), despite the distinct lack of sperm whales in the colonial interior. The editors of Byrd's commonplace book write that:

> [t]hese amplifications may strike some readers as affectedly erudite digressions, ranging as they do so far afield [. . .] However, they are not little modules of learning randomly inserted into the text: the amplifications function rhetorically to focus the reader's attention on certain themes, working from the commonly held principles of his time that human nature is essentially the same in all ages and places and that analogies and historic parallels aid understanding. (Berland et al. 40)

More simply, Richard Beale Davis writes that Byrd "ornaments his picture" in the *History* "with his learning and his knowledge or the world of men" (174).

These amplifications or ornaments often bring to the fore Byrd's participation in defining and extending the influence of empire. Throughout, there is the linear if difficult progress of the survey parties and the impact of colonialism on New World geography. In a form that is repeated over the length of the *History*, Byrd describes both the travails and the exact length of progress during a given period:

> In the mean while the Surveyors proceeded vigorously on their Business, but were so perplext with Thickets at their first setting off, that their Progress was much retarded.
>
> They were no sooner over that Difficulty, but they were oblig'd to encounter another. The rest of the day's-Work lay over very Sharp Hills, where the dry leaves were so slippery that there was hardly any hold for their feet. Such Rubbs as these prevented them from Measuring more than 4 Miles and 270 poles. (222)

In other areas of the text, he bemoans the apparent lack of interest in mapping geographical features that would improve England's strategic understanding of its colonial territories. Remarking on the paucity of information about the mountainous Blue Ridge area adjacent to the Shenandoah and James rivers, he writes, "It therefore concerns his Majesty's Service very nearly, and the Safety of His Subjects in this part of the World, to take Possession of so important a Barrier in time, lest our good Friends, the French, and the Indians, thro' their Means, prove a perpetual annoyance to these Colonies" (240).

In still other sections, patronizing of the colonized by the colonizer asserts itself, as does the use of the colonial landscape as food or sustenance for the home country. Donald Siebert notes that Byrd ranks Native Americans unfavorably with the despised Irish nationals (546), and Byrd's long translation of an explanation of Native American religious belief ends with the flat summation, "Indeed, the Indian Notion of a Future Happiness is a little Gross and Sensual, like Mahomet's Paradise. But how can it be otherwise, in a People that are contented with Nature as they find Her, and have no other Lights but what they receive from purblind Tradition?" (198-202). Moving to the landscape, descriptions of virtually every animal in the *History* include not simply physical and behavioral qualities but approximations of taste drawn from contemporary gastronomy. The oppossum is "well tasted and Tender, approaching nearest to Pig" (248), and the buffalo, or bison, must be related to regular cattle because "the Flesh of both has exactly the same taste" (288). Here we read not simply a bent toward realistic representation or designs for political geography but the reassurance that a colonial landscape and the things in it are meant ultimately for consumption by empire. Stephen Ausband writes that Byrd "[t]ypically [. . .] speculates on the potential usefulness" of what he finds (163-63), and this practice, underscored by Byrd's attitude toward indigenous peoples, anticipates what Mary Louise Pratt describes as a discourse of mastery common in nineteenth-century travel writing in the West.

The *Secret History*, on the other hand, is much more concerned with what might be called the "inside story" of the expedition. Percy Adams, Byrd's editor for the Dover parallel edition of the *History* and the *Secret History*, calls it the record of "controversies [. . .] gossip [. . .] sex [. . .] and scandal" (v) that attended and plagued the surveying effort. In this work, Byrd is more free in his tone and selection of material.

Stylistically, the more private narrative continues to show Byrd's wit and literary facility. The commissioners are given code names in the *Secret History*, a device that Adams relates to Byrd's familiarity with the Restoration comedy of manners, in which characters' names "revealed something" about them (xiii). It is a device which the editors of Byrd's commonplace book attribute to Byrd's understanding of the Theophrastan character sketch, a classical genre employed in seventeenth- and eighteenth-century English letters "either in the negative mode, casting telling characteristics of people [the writer] knew in a satirical light, or in the positive mode, praising one distinctive virtuous quality to form a eulogaic sketch" (Berland et al. 38-39). The result is a mix of literary reference and a tone sharper than that which Byrd deploys in the *History*. Biblical allusions abound in the *Secret History*, but their intent is more pointed. Byrd dubs survey parties who must bushwhack through the Great Dismal Swamp the "Dismalities," a satiric reference to Israel wandering in the wilderness more disrespectful than those in the *History*. With less interest in achieving a detached authorial stance, Byrd's comments are more immediate and involved, although the *Secret History* rises above the fully personal focus that Byrd engaged for his regular diaries. The *Secret History* was most likely meant to remain within an intimate circle of readers, the more so because it revealed, as Anderson notes, "the boundary commissioners' mixed performance of their duties" (702), and, as Siebert argues, Byrd's own "worrying over his role" in the expedition (538-41).

In terms of content, while the same events often appear in both histories, the rigorous delineation of each new phenomenon and the exhaustive physical detail of the *History* give way to tales of arguments among the commissioners; to running commentary on Byrd's own personal health, which often devolves into descriptions of emetics and purgatives he uses on himself and others; and to accounts of darker doings, including sexual advances on women that ranged from the strange to the dire. One commissioner picked scabs from a North Carolina woman whose disability prevented her from resisting. Byrd writes that "all she cou'd do, was, to sit stil, & make the Fashionable Exclamation of the Country, Flesh a live & tear it, & by what I understand she never spake so properly in her Life" (59). Shortly before this, while the surveying party was close enough to towns and hamlets to take lodging with private citizens, Byrd relates that some commissioners "broke the Rules of Hospitality, by several gross Freedoms they offer'd to take with our Landlord's Sister. She was indeed a pretty Girl, and therefore it was prudent to send her out of harm's Way" (53). Not blameless himself in treading over the line of propriety, Byrd's overstimulated interest in sex, a theme in his diary writing, kept the *Secret History* away from general readers, despite an interest expressed by Thomas Jefferson in publishing it. In contrast to the *History*, it was not thereafter considered for release until the early twentieth century (Adams xxi-xxii).

Although lighter in its emphasis on history, ethnography, and science, and perhaps less clearly implicated in the imperatives of empire, the *Secret History* nevertheless remains a close partner to the *History*. A great advantage to having recovered both narratives is the opportunity to lay them side by side. Anderson writes that "[t]he dividing line histories consistently provide material for dramatically contrasting treatments of the experiences that they record" (716), and William Boyd's 1929 edition of Byrd's works, on which the Dover parallel edition is based, allows readers the opportunity to compare how one event is treated differently in each history. It is the result of such comparison that brings travel writing in close relation to autobiography.

Travel Writing and Questions of Closure

Theorists of autobiography emphasize its indeterminacy. In a seminal work on autobiography, James Olney insists that "autobiography and poetry are both definitions of the self at a moment and in a place" (*Metaphors* 44). Later in his writing, he asserts "the impossibility of making any prescriptive definition for autobiography or placing any generic limitations on it at all" ("Some Versions" 237). In like fashion, Jean Starobinski writes that "it is essential to avoid speaking of an autobiographical 'style' or even an autobiographical 'form,' because there is no such generic style or form" (73). Louis Renza argues that "[p]erhaps more than any other literary concept, autobiography traps us into circular explanations of its being" (1).

Yet in trying to say what autobiography may be like, Renza proposes that "autobiography is neither fictive nor non-fictive, not even a mixture of the two. We might view it instead as a unique, self-defining mode of self-referential expression, one that allows, then inhibits, the project of self-presentification, of converting oneself into the present promised by language" (22). For Renza, there is no possibility of closure in autobiography, as autobiography does not structure itself in the self-contained world of fiction or the teleological world of history. "[W]e might conceive of autobiographical writing as an endless prelude," he writes, with deliberate reference to Wordsworth's autobiographical poem. It is "a beginning without middle (the realm of fiction), or without end (the realm of history); a purely fragmentary, incomplete literary project, unable to be more than an arbitrary document" (22).

While DeMan's analysis echoes Renza's in its conclusions about autobiography and closure, DeMan does not remove autobiography from comparison with fiction. Indeed, he writes that distinguishing autobiography from fiction is impossible. The concept of "concomitance" or "right *timing*" causes doubt as to whether circumstances have been manipulated to produce effects within a text (DeMan 921; emphasis original). From concomitance extend questions of truth or untruth, the positive or the privative. Following the dour assessment of language and meaning that marks his works in critical theory, DeMan concludes, "To the extent that language is figure [. . .] it is indeed not the thing itself but the representation, the picture of the thing and, as such, it is silent, mute as pictures are mute. Language, as trope, is always privative" (930).

Together, Byrd's histories provide close examples of both concomitance and the ultimate problem of representation articulated by DeMan. Of course, anxiety about a relative level of truth in travel writing is not new. The publisher of *Typee: or a Peep at Polynesian Life* pushed its author on that same question nearly a century after Byrd had begun writing his histories, finally to have Herman Melville famously ask, "After all, what is truth?" But as scholarship strives to define travel writing in contrast to other genres, it must keep in mind that, at its core, travel writing shares and enlarges upon the struggle with closure in which autobiography is engaged.

Take for instance an occurrence in early October 1728, about a month into the survey, in which Richard Fitz-William, one of Byrd's fellow commissioners from Virginia, shot and killed what was most likely a bob-cat (Ausband 85). Byrd relates the incident this way in the *History*:

> Some of our People had Shot a great Wild Cat, which was that fatal moment making a comfortable Meal upon a Fox-Squirrel, and an Ambitious Sportsman of our Company claim'd the merit of killing this monster after it was dead.
>
> The Wild-cat is as big again as any Household-Cat, and much the fiercest Inhabitant of the Woods. Whenever 'tis disabled, it will tear its own Flesh for madness. Altho' a Panther will run away from a Man, a Wild-cat will make only a Surly Retreat, now and then facing about, if he be too closely pursued; and will even pursue in his turn, if he observe the least Sign of Fear or even of caution in those that pretend to follow Him.
>
> The Flesh of this Beast, as well as the Panther, is as white as veal, and altogether as sweet and delicious. (164-166)

The passage articulates a familiar pattern in Byrd's description of the natural world. Whether the thing discovered be animal, vegetable, or human being, delineation of a particular incident, such as finding a bob-cat eating in the forest, quickly expands to treatment of a general subject or class. Here Byrd begins by describing a single animal but moves swiftly to a more general description of the species, abstracting the cat in larger discussions of behavior and culinary use. The second and third paragraphs are obviously composed of material gathered elsewhere, or at another time, the parts of the text that Adams calls "afterthoughts and information not available on the spot" (v) and that the editors of Byrd's commonplace book and Davis attribute to the historical and social outlooks of Byrd's time.

However, such secondary material performs a specific function in travel writing and particularly in travel writing so concerned with natural history and the natural world. Not simply would an audience expect it, especially the Royal Society audience to which Byrd may have been writing, but, as Janet Giltrow, James Jubak, and John Samson argue in separate studies of Anglo-American travel writing, information and comments that appear to go beyond a travel writer's immediate experience act as a check on the author's veracity. They validate reports drawn from personal observation (Giltrow 19-20; Jubak 128; Samson 4) and ensure an author's control over raw subject matter and the resulting text. While these arguments are centered on nineteenth-century texts, they certainly apply to texts written in the eighteenth century and before. Not simply an expression of literary learning or a neoclassic worldview, secondary information is integral to travel literature in that it supports a writer's claim to authenticity. Without an authoritative voice, travel narrative becomes something else—fiction, fantasy, romance.

The *Secret History* relates the encounter with the cat quite differently: "By the way Firebrand [Byrd's satiric codename for Fitz-William] had another Occasion to show his Prowess, in killing a poor little Wild Cat, which had been crippled by 2 or 3 before. Poor Puss was unhappily making a meal on a Fox Squirrel when all these misfortunes befell her" (165). The *History*, written in a gentlemanly, disinterested narrative voice, pictures the cat as an exaggerated, exotic animal. Byrd calls it large, or "great," and refers to it as a "monster," identifying it as an extraordinary creature. Its meal is a "comfortable" one, indicating that the bob-cat is at leisure in the forest, which is the site of much difficulty and danger for the men of the surveying party; Byrd tells often of surveyors becoming lost and spending cold or wet nights without food. This difference between the ordinary or known is repeated in Byrd's general description of the "wild cat" species. It is larger than the felines to which his potential audience would have been accustomed, and it is more strange and fierce still than the panther, which functions in the narrative as Byrd's standard for dangerous cats. There is a reference to "madness," to self-cannibalism, and to the disconcerting ability to sense fear and turn pursuer into pursued. In short, the cat leaps out of the forest bigger than life, an exhibit and a thrill for Byrd's prospective readers.

The private account shows the cat completely changed. Rather than a monster, it becomes a pitiful beast, "crippled" by an onslaught of rifle fire from the expedition. It is transformed from "big" to "little," from "great" to "poor"; its meal becomes unhappy instead of "comfortable." Rather than draw a distinction in size between bob-cats and house cats, as he does in the *History*, Byrd names the forest cat in the secret account "Poor Puss," granting it an endearment applied to domestic cats and, therefore, causing it to seem a close and unfortunate relative to them. The animal in the *Secret History* is almost unrecognizeable as the one depicted in the *History*, save for its common name and the type of squirrel it ate.

Byrd made these choices deliberately, to cover some uncomfortable circumstances revealed in the private narrative. In the *Secret History*, Byrd makes it clear that he despised Fitz-William, something better left unsaid in a document prepared for polite or general publication. Only a touch of this feeling appears in the *History*—the epithet "Ambitious Sportsman" is obviously ironic—but it blends easily into the detached style of the public document. In fact, Byrd hated Fitz-William on a number of accounts, and the more immediate and personal style of the *Secret History* allows his emotions almost full reign. As Boyd writes, Fitz-William, while he lived in Virginia and represented it in the survey, sided with North Carolina in arguments over tobacco trafficking and often supported its commissioners in disagreements during the expedition (Byrd 15n). Byrd, a loyal Virginian, took an immediate dislike to these politics. To compound the problem, it appears at least from Byrd's perspective that Fitz-William was also very difficult to get along with. Byrd reports in the *Secret History* that Fitz-William was an intemperate and unbearable traveling companion who forced himself on women (Fitz-William was the scab-picker and more) and argued with Byrd at every turn. He drank too much, took grand credit for even the smallest achievements, and kept the rest of the party awake by snoring and swearing in his sleep. The passage about wild cats in the *History* does more than provide information and entertainment for an audience. It hides a nasty side to the expedition and allows Byrd to maintain his public calm.

The clear differences between Byrd's histories echo in the work of other travel writers. For instance, in the classic study *Orientalism*, Edward Said reveals an action like Byrd's, and a like motivation, in the travel narratives of Gérard de Nerval. Nerval, who lived in the first half of the nineteenth century, was celebrated as a poet and essayist but also as a scholar of Arabic cultures. His writings on the region were taken as authoritative by both the reading public and the French government. In the early 1840s, Nerval published a celebrated book of travel sketches, *Voyage en Orient*, as the triumphal record of his sojourn in the areas he had learned and written about in Europe. As with other professional scholars of the "Orient," in this case Egypt and the lands surrounding it, Nerval was "prepared for [his travel] by voluminous reading in the classics, modern literature, and academic Orientalism" (Said 180). Yet once he encountered his object of study, Nerval appears to have failed to understand it. As Said's analysis demonstrates, Nerval copied passages from earlier scholarly works, wholesale and without notice, into his own sketches of cultures in North Africa and the Middle East.

While known primarily as a poet, Nerval's stature among the European community of professional scholars known as "Orientalists" was such that he ought not to have lacked a way to interpret, or at least represent, Eastern cultures once he encountered them firsthand. Yet this may have been exactly what happened. Nerval cribbed what Said calls "large swatches" of a book entitled *An Account of Manners and Customs of the Modern Egyptians*, written by the Englishman Edward William Lane, considered an eminent authority in nineteenth-century European studies of the East, in an attempt to cover his own inability to come to terms with a physical "Orient." Said explains, "It is as if having failed both in his search for a stable Oriental reality and in his intent to give systematic order to his re-presentation of the Orient, Nerval was employing the borrowed authority of a canonized Orientalist text" (184).

Nerval would not have been the first to employ elements of another text in his own travel writing; borrowing is part of a travel writer's repertoire, falling loosely under Adams' terms "information not available on the spot." And, to be sure, Nerval's personal contact with North African and Middle Eastern cultures was truly a mess, a long and incoherent travel itinerary that left Nerval in poor physical health and suffering an intellectual confusion similar to that which attended his two sustained periods of madness. Such a state of affairs might have called for extra resources in writing his text. However, by quietly substituting material from Lane for his own experience, Nerval achieves much more. He saves himself from professional embarrassment, much as Byrd's generalizations about wild cats cover uncomfortable events in the boundary line expedition. Without shoring up by Lane's prose, Nerval's book would have read more like an erotic hallucination than the travel experiences of a respected Orientalist, something Nerval wanted to avoid (Said 182-83).

Fredric Jameson writes in *The Prison House of Language* that "[l]anguage has of necessity recourse to indirection, to substitution [. . .] it must replace [the] empty center of content with something else, and it does so either by saying what the content is like (metaphor), or describing its context and the contours of its absence, listing the things that border around it (metonymy)" (122-23). Each motion, a move away from closure or totality, a version of DeMan's assertion that language is not the thing itself but only a picture, may be seen in Byrd's and Nerval's narratives. In Byrd, metaphor appears in the *Secret History* where the bob-cat is analogized as "Poor Puss," employing all the associations that come from such comparison but making the cat itself invisible, an "empty center of content." Metonymy is mixed with metaphor in the *History* when Byrd's attempt to describe the bob-cat for readers is caught almost immediately in both analogy and context. The reference to size, the ranking of its ferocity relative to other forest animals, and its relationship to the panther all create a web of relationships and associations that displace the original cat, leaving the text to describe an animal that isn't quite there. As Jameson notes, "[T]he concepts of metaphor and metonymy cannot be isolated from each other and undergo a ceaseless metamorphosis from the one into the other" (123). At places in the *History*'s description of the cat, particularly the end, metaphoric terms surge up in a phrase like "white as veal, and altogether as sweet and delicious," flowing into and flowing from the contours of absence. The empty center of content is replaced by both context and analogy, a continuing action of displacement and substitution. Similarly, Nerval, unable to compose an adequate or coherent representation of foreign cultures, directs a reader away from the absence at the heart of his text by substituting Lane's work for his own.

The passages from Byrd's histories and Nerval's travel sketches state Jameson's problem of language in a more complicated way, calling attention to the writer as an added factor in the motions of indirection and substitution, particularly if we are able to look in two texts at once. If, for instance, passages from the *History* can be read as a stand-in, or substitution, for events related in the *Secret History*, then the sort of information common to travel narrative, particularly in the eighteenth and nineteenth centuries, acts itself in motions of indirection and substitution. Secondary information about the cat directs attention away from Byrd's personal reactions to Fitz-William even as it directs a reader's gaze away from the empty center of content that would be the cat itself. In each work, but also *between* each work, the bob-cat disappears, rendered invisible by the workings of language and by the rhetorical manipulations of Byrd.

A similar complication is apparent in Nerval's text. The passages from Lane divert attention from the difficulty of Nerval's personal reputation, and simultaneously they divert a reader from the empty center of Nerval's text.

In theorizing representation of the self in historical writing, Anthony Paul Kerby argues that "one does not report an already constituted meaning of the past; rather, one seeks a narrative that synthesizes the various threads of the past into a coherent and plausible account. Such plausibility may depend on factors (*e.g.*, future events) not at all present to the actors of the events being considered" (242). Applied to Byrd's and Nerval's travel writing, Kerby's statement shows, apart from the problem of language articulated by Jameson, that each narrative's claim to plausibility depends greatly on the exclusion of its companion or source. The description of the wild cat in Byrd's *History* may read as a coherent and plausible account of encountering such an animal only if it is not laid alongside the account in the *Secret History*. For that matter, the reverse is true. Nerval's descriptions of North Africa appear plausible and coherent until they are laid alongside the work in which they originated. Each narrative—the *History*, the *Secret History*, *Voyage en Orient*—struggles for totality or closure, only to be de-faced not simply within itself but by another version of itself.

Extending DeMan's analysis of autobiography, the question is indeed not which of Byrd's histories provides more reliable knowledge of the boundary line expedition or of whether Nerval's writing is a fair representation of Arabic cultures. Rather, it lies in how DeMan's argument about the impossibility of closure is reflected in the relationship between Byrd's two travel narratives, as well as within each work, or in the relationship between Nerval's and Lane's works, as these relationships are created, contextualized, and manipulated by Byrd and Nerval themselves.

Read with their companion texts, Byrd's and Nerval's writings supplement the problem of trope and representation by adding the agency of the writer to the impossibility of closure. If the nature of language presents this problem, as DeMan and Jameson argue, the actions of an author compound it, particularly in travel narrative. DeMan and Jameson describe the workings of language in terms of double gestures—the giving and taking away of significance, the movement between metaphor and metonymy. In travel writing we see perhaps a triple gesture, in which the giving and taking away by language of the written subject, defined as the journey and the encounters along the way, are themselves supplemented by another taking away, this time on the part of the writing subject, the author who manipulates material to maintain a narrative persona. This gesture both affiliates travel writing with autobiography and serves to distinguish it from autobiography, in recognition of the rhetorical forces that affect its own textual production.

A Figure for Travel Writing

DeMan argues that "[t]he dominant figure [. . .] of autobiographical discourse is [. . .] the prosopopeia" (927), as "the etymology of the trope's name, *prosopon poein*, [means] to confer a mask or face" (926). If one sets a mask upright and spins it on its vertical axis, one creates the effect produced by the whirlygig—a blurred alternating between face and de-face, between presence and absence, leaving autobiographical discourse incapable of fully representing its subject.

Speculating on the examples in Byrd's histories and those in Nerval's sketches, a dominant figure or image for travel writing might be, rather than a thing, the action of disappearing and being disappeared. As Joan Didion explains in her travel meditation *Salvador*, "'[D]isappear' is in Spanish both an intransitive and a transitive verb," allowing one to transliterate into English such phrases as "he has disappeared" and "he has been disappeared" (57). Figuring travel writing in this way is not meant to trivialize the original use to which Didion puts her observation, which is as a method for explaining the mechanisms of state-sponsored terror in El Salvador in the 1980s. Nor is it completely allied to theoretical arguments articulated by Jacques Derrida and Robert Cover linking language and violence, although a strong case is made by Said for Nerval's use of Lane's text lending credence to other, more fantastical, pictures of Arabic cultures that appeared in *Voyage en Orient*. The result was a continuance of centuries-old images, created in Western literature and thought, of Eastern peoples as figures of desire, perpetuating the oppressive, heavy-handed measures Westerners enacted upon encountering the physical beings behind these images (Said 182-83).

The flexibility of the Spanish verb, which articulation, Didion notes, does not exist regularly in English, illuminates the nexus of actions at work in Byrd's histories, in Nerval's text, and by implication in travel writing in general. In the example from Byrd, the bob-cat is a doubly disappearing and disappeared subject, vanishing as much by Byrd's deliberate compositional processes as by the nature of language. Language, as DeMan and Jameson show, causes the cat to disappear into indeterminacy; Byrd supplements this by disappearing it for his own ends. In the example from Nerval, the subject is human beings and culture, with the same results in the text and more unhelpful consequences in political and cultural realms.

The ground between language, subject, and writer, the place of disappearing/being disappeared, promises to serve as ground on which to establish for travel writing what DeMan would call a "model of cognition" (923). It is ground on which travel literature may be seen not simply as an object of study but, increasingly, as an important subject for theoretical dialogue. In a discussion of post-modern travel literature, Alison Russell argues that travel writing based in the style of Byrd's or Nerval's, while it continues to be practiced at the present time, is in danger of becoming an "exhausted" form:

> If people used to read travel narratives to educate themselves about the world or to experience a journey vicariously, the efficiency of modern transportation and the advent of cable television and other forms of electronic media would seem to make travel literature somewhat pointless: why read about someone else's trip to Italy when you can watch one on television or simulate it using the internet? In the past few decades, travel writers have been faced with a problem much like that of fiction writers of the same period: a sense of exhaustion of the planet and exhaustion of the forms we use to write about it. (8-9)

Russell notes that some travel writers have attempted to head off exhaustion by "undertak[ing] perilous journeys or choos[ing] the most circuitous routes or unusual modes of transportation" in retracing or revising authors' past journeys, or by organizing narratives around themes of popular culture, such as visits to baseball parks or sites important to fans of Elvis Presley (9-10). Whichever, the contemporary travel writer, influenced by post-modern experiments in fiction and by an increasing knowledge that self-conscious tourism is the post-modern mode for travel, seeks a distance from travel literature in earlier centuries, in order to maintain vitality within the literature itself and within individual expressions of that literature.

To view the anxiety evidenced by Byrd and Nerval in their self-presentation is to realize just how concerned each was with what John Urry calls the "constraints of high culture" (qtd. in Russell 7), in a way that many contemporary travel writers are not, even as each earlier author showed an ability to be absorbed into choice, play, and multiplicity in his texts. However, that anxiety can be viewed in relation to what Russell identifies as the "delight" of the post-tourist (7), who, according to Urry, knows that "tourism is a game, or rather a series of games with multiple texts and no single, authentic touristic experience" (qtd. in Russell 7). Such viewing opens an awareness of what Renza calls "self-presentification"—an identifying strand in a literature that, like Starobinski's description of autobiography, seems to resist generic contours (Van den Abbeele 9). The study of autobiography, according to Olney, has been "moving from a focus on 'bios,' or the course of a lifetime, to focus on 'autos,' the self writing and being written" (*Memory* xv). Indeed, it might be argued that, in many other manifestations of writing, a writer's strategies of self-presentification and degree of self-awareness have more clearly become subjects for critical study and scholarly debate.

Disappearing/being disappeared deepens travel literature's involvement in this important theoretical focus by tying together an evolution of self-awareness in travel literature, linking Byrd's and Nerval's periods with post-modern gestures toward representing travel. Whether the contemporary writer be someone like Bill Bryson, whom Russell notes is known for "relating his preference for hotels that get the BBC-1, his breaks for Cokes and meals at Pizza Hut, and his weakness for crummy Italian movies and tacky souvenirs" (10-11), or one of a group of writers whose "direct confrontation with the effects and politics of spatial exhaustion" causes them to focus their travel texts on a "solution to the crisis of global mismanagement" (18-19), heightened understanding of an author's self-presence in travel writing focuses a reader's attention on what may be disappeared, under whatever intent, for the sake of a narrative persona.

As scholarship in travel writing moves forward, this place between writing and being written, between disappearing and being disappeared, should become an important place of survey and analysis. By focusing more equally on writer and journey, criticism of travel narrative will be better able to participate in larger discussions about writing, about form or its absence, and about the problems of representation that plague all texts.

Works Cited

Adams, Percy. "Introduction to the Dover Edition." Introduction. *Histories of the Dividing Line Betwixt Virginia and North Carolina.* By William Byrd. Ed. William K. Boyd. New York: Dover, 1967. v-xxii.

Alami, Ahmed. "Discordant Evangelical Visions, Ideological Intent and the Construction of the Reader in James Richardson's *Travels in Morocco* (1860)." *English Studies: Working Papers on the Web: Representing Morocco* 7 (2004): 26 pars. 12 May 2005, <http://www.shu.ac.uk/wpw/morocco/Idrissi/Idrissi.htm>.

Anderson, Douglas. "Plotting William Byrd." *The William and Mary Quarterly* 56.4 (October 1999): 701-722.

Ausband, Stephen. *Byrd's Line: A Natural History.* Charlottesville: U of Virginia P, 2002.

Berland, Kevin, and Jan Kirsten and Kenneth Lockridge, eds. *The Commonplace Book of William Byrd of Westover.* Durham: U of North Carolina P, 2001.

Byrd, William. *Histories of the Dividing Line Betwixt Virginia and North Carolina.* Ed. William K. Boyd. New York: Dover, 1967.

Cover, Robert. "Violence and the Word." *Yale Law Journal* 95 (1986): 1601-29.

Croome, Richard. *William Byrd of Westover.* Boston: Houghton Mifflin, 1932.

Davis, Richard. "William Byrd: Taste and Tolerance." *Major Writers of Early American Literature.* Ed. Everett Emerson. Madison: U of Wisconsin P, 1972. 151-77.

DeMan, Paul. "Autobiography as De-Facement." *Modern Language Notes* 94.5 (1979): 919-30.
Derrida, Jacques. "The Force of Law: 'The Mystical Foundations of Authority.'" *Cardozo Law Review* 11.4-5 (1990): 919-1046.
Didion, Joan. *Salvador*. New York: Simon and Schuster, 1982.
Folks, Jeffrey. "Crowd Types in William Byrd's Histories." *Southern Literary Journal* 26.2 (Spring 1994): 3-10.
Giltrow, Janet. "Speaking Out: Travel and Structure in Herman Melville's Early Narratives." *American Literature* 52.1 (1980): 18-32.
Jameson, Fredric. *The Prison-House of Language*. Princeton: Princeton UP, 1972.
Jubak, James. "The Influence of Travel Narrative on Melville's *Mardi*." *Genre* 9 (1976): 121-33.
Kerby, Anthony. "The Adequacy of Self-Narration: A Hermenuetical Approach." *Philosophy and Literature* 12.2 (1988): 232-244.
Olney, James. *Memory and Narrative: The Weave of Life-Writing*. Chicago: U of Chicago P, 1998.
—. *Metaphors of the Self.* Princeton: Princeton UP, 1972.
—. "Some Versions of Memory/Some Versions of *Bios*: The Ontology of Autobiography." *Autobiography: Essays Theoretical and Critical*. Ed. James Olney. Princeton: Princeton UP, 1980. 236-67.
Pratt, Mary Louise. *Imperial Eyes and Transculturation*. New York: Routledge, 1992.
Renza, Louis. "The Veto of the Imagination: A Theory of Autobiography." *New Literary History* 9.1 (Autumn 1977): 1-26.
Russell, Alison. *Crossing Boundaries: Postmodern Travel Literature*. New York, Palgrave, 2000.
Said, Edward. *Orientalism*. New York, Vintage, 1978.
Samson, John. *White Lies: Melville's Narratives of Facts*. Ithaca: Cornell UP, 1989.
Siebert, Donald. "William Byrd's *Histories of the Line*: The Fashioning of a Hero." *American Literature* 47.4 (1976): 535-51.
Smith, David. "William Byrd Surveys America." *Early American Literature* 11 (1976/77): 296-310.
Starobinski, Jean. "The Style of Autobiography." Trans. Seymour Chatman. *Autobiography: Essays Theoretical and Critical*. Ed. James Olney. Princeton: Princeton UP, 1980. 73-83.
Van den Abbeele, Georges. "Sightseers: The Tourist as Theorist." *Diacritics* 10.4 (1980): 2-14.
Wright, Louis. Introduction. *The Prose Works of William Byrd of Westover*. Ed. Louis Wright. Cambridge: Harvard UP, 1966. 1-35.

CHAPTER FIVE

E. J. PRATT'S *BRÉBEUF AND HIS BRETHREN*: MAPPING THE MARTYRS' SHRINE IN POETIC PILGRIMAGE

SHOSHANNAH GANZ

Brébeuf and His Brethren is a poem concerned with a faith journey that, while the result of a missionary call, is in many ways what Victor and Edith Turner refer to as a "charter pilgrimage," laying the groundwork for both Catholic pilgrimage and a poetry that deals with the root of pilgrimage: the emulation of Christ's journey and the active faith journey of the participants. *Brébeuf and His Brethren* was written in 1940, inspired by the massive works of Pelham Edgar on the Jesuit missions and by the source material in *The Jesuit Relations*, first published in France from 1632 to 1673. These letters, written by the Jesuit fathers who were working in the mission fields of what later became Canada, record their journeys through the wilderness and their interaction with the five indigenous tribes that made up the Wendat nation (later named the Hurons by the French). While evidence and writing about the site of the Jesuit mission (called Sainte-Marie among the Hurons) and about the nearby site of the martyrdom of Brébeuf and other Jesuit priests dates back to as early as the mid-nineteenth century, it was not until 1940, when the site came back into the hands of the Jesuits, that real interest was revived in preserving, excavating, and memorializing these mission and martyrdom sites.

E. J. Pratt's *Brébeuf and His Brethren* (1940) has, like many pilgrimage sites and foundation narratives, become itself a contested site of historical, literary, and theological or religious authority. The overwhelming emphasis in the critical discussions of this poem focuses on issues outside the text of the poem, drawing on other writings of Pratt and on the biographical details of his life in order to support or discredit readings of the poet as "purely humanistic," as being in a crisis of faith, as atheistic, as agnostic, or, as Pelham Edgar suggests, as "a Protestant poet [who] writes the greatest Catholic poem of our day" (qtd. in Wilson 58).[1] In fact, Angela T. McAuliffe, in *Between the Temple and the*

Cave: The Religious Dimensions of the Poetry of E. J. Pratt, goes so far as to suggest an "Ignatian spirituality" (187) in the poet that she describes earlier as a "Wesleyan Methodist by upbringing" only (187). Peter Hunt, following on the work of a variety of critics who make these claims as to the faith inclinations or disinclinations of the poet, presented a paper at the University of Ottawa's 1977 Pratt Symposium (later published as part of the *ReAppraisals* series) that looks at the critical work surrounding *Brébeuf and His Brethren*, claiming that the poem is "largely misinterpreted by the critics" (Hunt 69).[2] Rather than entering into a debate of this nature and involving either myself or the poet in a struggle for religious or theological definition, it will suffice to note that this poem and poet, like the Father/Saint Augustine who is claimed by both the Catholics and Protestants, are claimed by many different traditions of belief. The poem appeals to the varieties of faith experience and belief through an enlivening historical re-telling of one of the foundation narratives and pilgrimages of Canadian letters and history. In part, Pratt himself responds to questions regarding his religious orientation with these words: "whether one is Protestant or Catholic, one may feel as I did when I stood with Mr. Wilfrid Jury, the archaeologist, within a few feet of the place where Brébeuf offered up his life. It was indeed sacred ground" (qtd. in Gingell, *Collected Works* xxix).[3]

While I have taken some pains to mention the critical debates of the past twenty years surrounding E. J. Pratt, particularly with regards to the religious orientation of the poet, the spiritual journey or pilgrimage of the poet himself is only of interest in so much as it can be seen to have influenced his understanding of Brébeuf and his creation of this poetic persona. In fact, I will be giving a great deal more attention to the poetic process of the poet, a pilgrimage of sorts, that Pratt himself looked to as both source and inspiration for his writing. In this case the document that will be under examination is the actual memorial site and martyrs' shrine in Midland, Ontario. This site becomes the source for topographical, geographical, anthropological, religious, and historical information that can be mapped through the poem. I will first introduce the poet's experience of visiting the site, engage in a "close reading" of the site, and show the relevance of this site to the pilgrimage process and experience of the poem.

Pratt's upbringing and early adult experience inspired in him an interest in sacred callings and pilgrimage. As the son of a missionary and later as an out-port preacher for the Methodist church, he was intimately involved in activities of faith and the experience of faith journeys. Quoting Pratt, David G. Pitt writes that Pratt thought of his father as "a bit of the saint and a lot of the martyr" (*E. J. Pratt: The Truant Years* 4) and as "a sainted fallen warrior" (*E. J. Pratt: The Truant Years* 69). Angela McAuliffe remembers Pratt as "another John the Baptist, 'a burning and shining light' (John 5:35), by which 'many were enabled to find their way to the cross, and to the City of God'" (McAuliffe 5). On his memorial plaque, the connection between E. J. Pratt's father and the founding Father of the Catholic tradition and pilgrimage in Canada is made even more explicit: "[John Pratt] alone was destined to fall at his post during the first century of Methodism in Newfoundland" (McAuliffe 5). Describing E. J. Pratt's ministry, Pitt writes: "often he had to preach three times on a Sunday and walk fifteen miles, frequently in the vilest of weather, to complete his round of pulpits. It was a baptism of fire" (*E.J. Pratt: The Truant Years* 70). Undoubtedly the poet's own "faith" journeys and the model of his father as a martyr and a saint contributed to his vision of the Jesuit pilgrimage and to the character of the sainted martyr, Brébeuf. Surely E. J. Pratt's earliest years of schooling in the Christian faith, although not in the Catholic tradition, had a great deal to do with his later vision of the instruction of the Hurons in the Christian faith by the Jesuit fathers. Pratt describes his experience: "Oh, the preaching I listened to as a boy! We got heaven and hell drummed into us. At seven or eight years of age, I listened to the actual crackling of flames" (Gingell, *Collected Works* 42). Later, drawing from his early experience with death in the treacherous seas of the out-port communities, he questioned the message of God's goodness in light of the fact of human suffering, which led him on a quest not unlike a pilgrimage for an understanding of truth. Pratt writes, "We were brought up in the belief of the goodness of God and yet we had to reconcile tragedy with it. We were always under that shadow" (Gingell, *Collected Works* 43).

In the years that followed, Pratt went on to study for the ministry at the University of Toronto, where he engaged with the life and works of Paul, a figure who in many ways, like his own father, can be seen to resemble the sacrificial figure of Brébeuf. In "Studies in Pauline Eschatology and Its Background," Pratt closely examines the following verses written by Paul to the Romans: "For if we become united with him in the likeness of his death, we shall be also in the likeness of his resurrection" (Romans 6:5) and "If so be that we suffer with him, that we may be also glorified with him" (Romans 8:17). Writing of Paul, he presents a vision of a missionary figure with methods much like those of his later poetic reconstruction of Brébeuf. Pratt writes:

> His method is not that of a theorist who wishes to construct a view of the universe that might satisfy a logical test, but that of a missionary who brought a practical ingenuity to bear upon the multifarious moral and social needs that grew in proportion to the expansion of his churches, and demanded sometimes immediate adjustments [...] And to accomplish this, he adopted the customs, modes of thought, and phraseology native to the peoples amongst whom he laboured. (Gingell, *E. J. Pratt: Pursuits* 32-33)

While it is clear that for E. J. Pratt the writing of this poem was a quest—one that was invested with the colors of his early instruction in the Christian faith, the example of his father, his own arduous journeys while working as a preacher, and his earlier work on Paul and interest in sacrifice—it is most clearly in the poem itself, with its sacred callings and journeys, that he gives a picture of the faith invested in the founding pilgrimage story of Brébeuf and the other Jesuit fathers. S. H. Soper describes E. J. Pratt (known to Soper and other friends as Ned) as follows: "I think it can be said that Ned Pratt set out on a kind of quest, which had as its goal nothing less than Truth—with a capital T" (Pitt, *E. J. Pratt: The Truant Years* 87). He concludes, "I am sure he realized that the truth might turn out to be a rather bleak affair, but that didn't deter him" (Pitt, *E. J. Pratt: The Truant Years* 87). Indeed Pratt writes of his own journey from out of the shadow of meaningless death of fishers in the out-port communities of Newfoundland to an understanding of sacrifice: "This constitutes the main problem for idealistic literature: to get the anomalies explained, to find a place for man in a setting that makes sense to our baffled understanding, and the more we find ourselves in the presence of sacrificial deeds, the closer we get to the heart of life and the heart of the universe" (Gingell, *Collected Works* xxxvi). Indeed, the connection between faith and sacrifice is explicit in the lives of the earliest Jesuits:

> Brébeuf and Lalemant wished for death. They had asked themselves long before: Shall I go through with this mission work in New France and take everything that's coming, or not? They were continually putting themselves into a condition of capture. They knew death by hatchets would come someday. There was an ecstasy in their hearts at the time of death. (Gingell, *Collected Works* 47)

Brébeuf's letter of 1635, published in *The Jesuit Relations* and quoted by the poet "to loom in history" (Pratt, *Brébeuf and His Brethren* 114), calls for more labourers in the fields of New France and exults in the suffering of the journey and life in the colony. Writing from a tabernacle grove in the midst of winter, Pratt's Brébeuf writes: "To share our labours, come; for you will find / A consolation in the cross that far outweighs / Its burdens" (Pratt, *Brébeuf and His Brethren* 114). The path of the pilgrim is, indeed, filled with miracles to compensate for the struggles and suffering of the road. As Turner and Turner, Alan Morinis, Simon Coleman and John Elsner, and others have shown, most world religions and, particularly, the Catholic pilgrimage, involve encounters with supernatural beings. In Catholic pilgrimage, the main figures of supernatural encounter are Mary, Christ, the Cross, the prophets, and the apostles. Jean de Brébeuf had visions of the cross, and his visions of Mary are memorialized in a prayer garden at the site of his martyrdom. These visions are placed by the poet alongside those of biblical letter-writers and missionaries:

The priest would wander to the pines and build
His oratory where celestial visions
Sustained his soul. As unto Paul and John
Of Patmos and the martyr multitude
The signs were given—voices from the clouds,
Forms that illumined darkness, stabbed despair,
Turned dungeons into temples and a brand
Of shame into the ultimate boast of time—
So to Brébeuf had Christ appeared and Mary.
—Pratt, *Brébeuf and His Brethren* 115

Alan Morinis writes in the introduction to *Sacred Journeys: The Anthropology of Pilgrimage* that "Pilgrimage is inclined to vows and promises because the solutions to the seemingly insurmountable difficulties that motivate a sacred journey must come from a higher order of power" (27). Indeed, after his encounter with Mary and Christ, Brébeuf has an experience similar to the "call" and "command" of Saint Augustine under the pear tree, which figures as the story of Augustine's conversion in *The Confessions*. However, for Brébeuf this is not the Augustinian or Pauline converting voice of God but is a pilgrimage command like the one heard by Moses and Jonah. The command of God is then associated by Pratt with Brébeuf's subsequent pilgrimage vow. Pratt writes: "One night at prayer he heard a voice command— / *'Rise, Read!'* Opening the *Imitatio Christi,* / His eyes *'without design'* fell on the chapter, / *Concerning the royal way of the Holy Cross*, / Which place upon his spirit *'a great peace'* (Pratt, *Brébeuf and His Brethren* 115). In the passage that follows, the miraculous reenactment of the Augustine experience or perhaps even Paul's Damascus road experience, Brébeuf makes a vow to follow the path of Christ and continue on the pilgrim's road:

And then, day having come, he wrote his vow—
'*My God, my Saviour, I take from thy hand*
The cup of thy sufferings. I invoke thy name;
I vow never to fail thee in the grace
Of martyrdom, if by thy mercy, Thou
Dost offer it to me. I bind myself,
And when I have received the stroke of death,
I will accept it from thy gracious hand
With all pleasure and with joy in my heart;
To thee my blood, my body and my life'.
—Pratt, *Brébeuf and His Brethren* 115

Brébeuf's encounters with Mary, the Cross, and Christ, and the resulting vow that he took to give his life, body, and spirit to the mission fields and, eventually, to martyrdom, are all memorialized in various paintings, statuary, plaques, stained-glass windows, and in excerpts from *The Jesuit Relations* at the martyrs' shrine in Midland, Ontario. The shrine site was visited by E. J. Pratt during his research for the writing of *Brébeuf and His Brethren*, and he later translated Brébeuf's experiences and writings into his 1940 long poem, *Brébeuf and His Brethren.*

As a prelude to exploring the sacred site that inspired Pratt's poetry, it is important to understand the theoretical importance of this exploration in terms of the anthropology of pilgrimage. Victor and Edith Turner, the most prominent anthropologists and scholars in the area of pilgrimage, characterize this journey as follows:

> Pilgrimage is one way, perhaps the most literal, of imitating the religious founder. By visiting the sites believed to be the scenes of his life and teaching mission, the pilgrim in imagination relives those events. (33)

They go on to conclude that "pilgrimage may be thought of as extroverted mysticism, just as mysticism is introverted pilgrimage" (Turner and Turner 33). While the Turners discuss the mystical aspects of pilgrimage, Alan Morinis tries to break down these aspects of the mystical into components that contribute to what he calls "spiritual magnetism," the quality that draws the pilgrims to the actual site of pilgrimage, the place where the events discussed by the Turners are repeated or re-enacted in particular ways. Morinis writes that "Places of pilgrimage are endowed with spiritual magnetism by association with (1) miraculous cures, (2) apparitions of supernatural beings, (3) sacred geography, (4) [and] difficulty of access" (33). Morinis proceeds to suggest that "there is something energizing about locations where encounters with deities once happened, even though these events may have taken place thousands of years ago" (34).

E. J. Pratt's creative process in the writing of the long poem *Brébeuf and His Brethren* takes place in what could be considered reverse order. He starts with the ending and works his way to the beginning, in pilgrimage terms reversing the journey, beginning with the sacred site and moving toward the point of origin. In "A Profile of a Canadian Poet," Pratt says, "Always in my mind is the importance of having the ending right; that's the reason why I write the end first" (Gingell, *Collected Works*18), and later in the same talk he describes the process as follows: "I gradually weave my way back to the beginning" (Gingell, *Collected Works* 18).

In "Spiritual Magnetism," James J. Preston suggests that "pilgrimage sites are often found in the most dramatic locations on the globe and inspire lofty emotions and high spiritual values" (35). Sacred sites such as Mecca, Rome, and Jerusalem are "located at the crossroads of previous civilizations that have been transformed and synthesized time and again into new world views by saints and prophets" (Preston 35). These places of cultural and faith transformation become the "focal points for movements of large numbers of people towards centers of civilization" (Preston 35). E. J. Pratt was acutely aware of how important it was to pay attention to geography, architecture, and topography in recounting the foundation pilgrimage or charter narrative of the earliest Canadian pilgrims. He writes that he made "a number of visits to the shrines and the sites of the ancient missions to get some knowledge of the topography, of the flora and fauna, of the rocks and trees, the trails, the waterways, the edible roots, and the proper names, personal and geographical" (Gingell, *Collected Works* xxiv). Indeed, one component that seems particularly important in the charter journey of Brébeuf and the other Jesuits is the difficulty of access to what became the site of their martyrdom and was initially a site established at the crossroads of traditional Huron culture and French imperial expansion (both temporal and spiritual).

In order to reconstruct the sacred site that would later become a Canadian pilgrimage site, it was necessary for Pratt first to find the traces of this pilgrimage both in the literature of early Canada and in the land. Preston discusses the way of connecting through what he calls the "sacred trace":

> The phenomena of an invisible reality made visible in the world is what I call the sacred trace. Trace is defined in the dictionary "as a visible mark or sign of the former presence or passage of some person, thing or event." It also means, in its archaic usage, "a path or trail through a wilderness." [...] The sacred trace is located at the core of every pilgrimage. It takes many different forms. In some cases it is the relics or tomb of a saint; it may be the place where Muhammad delivered his sermon, calling together the Brotherhood of Islam or where Jesus of Nazareth rose from the dead. The trace is the source of spiritual magnetism of a shrine, its power house, so to speak. By participating in the epiphany manifested at a particular place of pilgrimage, the pilgrim ingests and carries home the trace of his tradition, then anchors or implants it in his home community. This is part of the reason why sacred objects (sacramentals) of all sorts are purchased and brought home from pilgrimage shrines. (41)

Pratt's own early experience of faith and death in the colony of Newfoundland is everywhere compared with his experience of working on the trace narratives in the land and the literatures of the North American Jesuit mission: "The search for the lost is particularly a characteristic of the Newfoundland tradition as it is part of the Christian tradition" (Gingell, *Collected Works* 18). At the "core" of the sacred journey of Pratt and Brébeuf, is the spiritual magnetism of the site at which Brébeuf and other Jesuit priests were martyred. This site is also marked by the relics of these early pilgrimages, by the encounters of Brébeuf with Christ and Mary and by visions, miracles, and what could be considered the daily martyrdom of the Jesuits in the camps of the Hurons.

The sacred traces that Pratt started with at the pilgrim site in Midland, Ontario allow the poet to work backwards through the entire sacred journey. Indeed, when writing of the site, Pratt imaginatively draws from the traces of those early journeys. In the final passage of *Brébeuf and His Brethren*, the poet writes:

> The trails, having frayed the threads of the cassocks, sank
> Under the mould of the centuries, under fern
> And brier and fungus – there in due time to blossom
> Into the highways that lead to the crest of the hill
> Which havened both shepherd and flock in the days of trial. (Pratt 151)

In the "shepherd and flock" of the pastoral scene of this pilgrimage site, Pratt appeals to one of the recurring pilgrimage motifs of Catholic tradition. Turner and Turner show that most foundation narratives include the pastoral elements of the foundational narrative of the Christ story—shepherds seeing the sacred signs and being led to an encounter with the divine. Turner and Turner, writing about what they call the "shepherd component," connect this aspect of pilgrimage explicitly with "the charter narrative of the Birth of Christ in Luke 2:7-20" (42). The idea of this biblical motif, as it occurs and influences the later cycles of sacred journey, is summed up as follows:

> shepherds have a vision (of 'an angel of the Lord'), and go on a kind of pilgrimage to witness the 'sign' (the infant Jesus laid in a manger, traditionally in a cave), and to pay their respects to the holy family. An Old Testament prototype was the peregrination of Abraham, the pastoral nomad and exile seeking Canaan. (Turner and Turner 42)

While in the days of "their trial" the sacred site of the Jesuit martyrdom "havened both shepherd and flock," thus invoking this pastoral motif of both foundation narrative and later charter narratives in the pilgrimage tradition, Pratt's description of the martyrs' shrine also gives detailed topographical description of the actual wilderness setting of this scene. This occurs in the first lines of the poem and again in the final verses, in his description of the "winds of God" that blew through France and are now

> Blowing once more through the pines
> That bulwark the shores of the great Fresh Water Sea.
> Over the wastes abandoned by human tread,
> Where only the bittern's cry was heard at dusk;
> Over the lakes where the wild ducks built their nests.
> —Pratt, *Brébeuf and His Brethren* 150

This inspiring wind leads to the fire of the martyrs, the Hurons, and to the starry expanse of the skies, where even now the traces of this pilgrimage are found in the agricultural motif here invoked in relation to the martyrs: "The years as they turned have ripened the martyrs' seed" (Pratt, *Brébeuf and His Brethren* 150). All of this seeds the foundation of the sacred site and martyrs' shrine in Midland, Ontario, and seeding later figures in the agricultural metaphor of missionary conquest.

As E. J. Pratt began his work with a study of the martyrs' shrine, so too my research includes a careful examination of the topographical, architectural, and touristic elements of the martyrs' shrine in Midland, Ontario and of the reconstructed fort across Ontario Highway 12, just outside of Midland of Saint-Marie Among the Hurons. A descriptive topographical analysis of this fort is helpful in understanding both Pratt's vision and those elements of the site that likewise commemorate the lives and mission of the Jesuits and the Huron people.

The sacred architecture of the cathedral itself is likely to hold the pilgrim in awe upon first arrival to the site. I visited the site on 4 October 2004, a sunny, autumn day when the streaming sunlight reflected the brilliant colors of the fall leaves and shone through the sacred scenes of the cathedral windows. Massimo Centini, discusses the importance of elevation in sacred architecture:

> the theme of elevation [is] reflected in religious architecture. From the menhir to the pyramid, from the ziggurat to the stupa, to the steeples of our churches, the desire to erect a structure able to form a "connection" between earth and heaven is striking. It marks the continuation of an iconographic tradition which makes no concession to symbolism but has instead maintained its profundity since ancient times. (Centini qtd. in Swatos 11) [4]

The road to the shrine winds up a fairly steep incline with large steps leading up to the cathedral; the rising pathway is flanked on either side by statues of the first two Jesuit Canadian martyrs, Saint Isaac Jogues and Saint Noel Chabanel, with the first native martyr, Catherine Tekakwitha, off to the right under a flaming maple tree near the shrine gift shop and cafeteria. As Centini observes, elevation is a part of the majesty of both the architecture of the cathedral and the natural setting. The eyes of the pilgrim are always being drawn heavenward, sweeping up the hill to the cathedral steps, up the steps to the cathedral, and up the cathedral to the towering double steeples and the heavens above. The journey up the hillside and steps leaves the pilgrim breathless at the entrance to the cathedral.

The thirty-seven sites on a clearly marked map of the site begin with a visit to The Shrine Church, built in 1926. Elaborate baroque paintings of the Stations of the Cross lead the pilgrim around the perimeter of the cathedral. Beginning on the right of the door there are guides for the pilgrim in languages ranging from native Ojibway, Japanese, Italian, Hungarian and the two official Canadian languages, English and French. Interspersed between the painted depictions of the Stations of the Cross are stained glass windows depicting vignettes such as the native Saint Catherine Tekakwitha or Brébeuf meeting with Chiwatenhwa. As the pilgrim's eyes move up the cathedral's walls to the colored light streaming through the high windows of the cathedral, one sees the eight Jesuit martyrs this site was established to commemorate depicted in stained glass, raising their hands to the light of God. To the right and left of the altar are the crypts of Lalemant and Brébeuf, followed by a reliquary containing their remains and the relics of Brébeuf's skull and the bones of other martyrs. Over the altar is a painting showing the eight martyrs joined together like dark Jesuit angels, administering the sacraments and presiding under Christ and over the congregation at the altar.

Exiting the cathedral on the left, the pilgrim's gaze is again drawn upward, toward a shrine to Our Lady of Huronia and upward again toward a fountain honouring St. Joseph and through bronze statuary Stations of the Cross. The fourteen stations lead the pilgrim up the mountain side under a cathedral of maple trees. At the top of the hill is a wooden structure that looks somewhat like a lookout. Upon arrival the pilgrim reads a plaque in the two official languages that suggests that this would, indeed, have been a lookout spot for the Hurons and French of Fort Saint Marie—a point from which they could see the trade routes, watch for marauding enemies, and generally see the spread of waterways and Georgian Bay. Today this point looks out over the town of Midland and over the sprawl of highways and industry scarring the landscape. Gazing back at the martyr's site, the pilgrim looks down on the Stations of the Cross and across a field of simple wooden crosses to an open-air cathedral, the site of Pope John Paul II's visit in 1984, which contains a painting of the eight martyrs much like the one in the cathedral part way up the hill. Descending from the lookout, the pilgrim can gain closer inspection of the open-air cathedral by winding through the wooden crosses scattered across the field. Turning back toward the highway, the pilgrim can begin the descent down the hillside, this time stopping at Brébeuf's prayer garden, said to be the site of his visions of Mary and the martyrdom cross—a quiet place surrounded by the wild growth of late autumn forest and foliage. Emerging from this quiet place, the pilgrim will again pass the final Stations of the Cross, ending up near the gift shop and canteen.

Many of the sites above and below the cathedral, including those on the apex of the hill, are shrines for various ethnic groups in Canada. These include: Our Lady of Czestochowa outdoor altar (Polish), Fatima Shrine (Portuguese), First Nations Park, Ukrainian Shrine, Slovak Cross, St. Lorenzo Ruiz Shrine (Filipino), Belarusian Cross, Holy Crucifixion Shrine (Community of S. Nicola da Crissa), Holy Family Shrine (Italian), Slovenian Cross, St. John Neumann Shrine (German), and an Irish Peace Garden. Likewise the site also commemorates not only the martyrdom of the first Jesuits and Native converts but also the history of the Jesuit movement and the contemporary Catholic involvement. There is the St. Ignatius Prayer Room, statuary of St. Francis of Assisi, and stained glass of warrior-priest Loyola. There is also a Papal Altar, a Papal Visit Monument, and a Wood carving of Pope John Paul II. The gift shop is filled with commemorative statues and pendants of the martyr saints and with contemporary literature in various languages on all aspects of the Catholic faith.

The pilgrim now has the choice of driving across the highway to the reconstructed fort or of following the walkway by the river, under the highway and past the grave of Brébeuf. On my visits, school groups and tourists often visited the reconstructed village without crossing the highway to the site of the martyrs' graves or shrine. The sacred journey around the Stations of the Cross that ends and begins with the marks of consumerism are even more evident in the overtly touristic character of the reconstructed village. In fact, it has been suggested that "tourism and pilgrimage are forged together, amplified, and orchestrated to reinforce nationalistic/ethnic identities" (Preston 36).

The site of the village of Sainte-Marie Among the Hurons is the place where the excavation activities supported by the University of Western Ontario in the 1940s took place, a process which E. J. Pratt himself witnessed in the uncovering of the layers of the village intermixed with the Jesuit relics. Every visit to Sainte-Marie Among the Hurons begins with an educational video that outlines the history of the fort as a trade post, a Christian settlement, and a garrison in the midst of warring tribes. The contact between the Jesuits and the Wendat people (as they called themselves), the five tribes that came under the French name of Hurons, is shown in staged video footage and excerpts from *The Jesuit Relations*. The fort itself shows the Church of Saint Joseph and the native church, the living quarters of the soldiers and priests, the Christian Longhouse and wigwams, and the traditional Wendat quarters, while also highlighting the agricultural activities area, livestock area, fleshing area, granary, carpentry shop, blacksmith shop, waterways, tailor/shoemaker shop, apothecary, and hospital. School groups are instructed in the way of life of the priests and Natives, and guides dressed in native and Jesuit attire talk to the tourists and are on hand for photographing. However, when E. J. Pratt began his research, the village was only under initial consideration as the site of an archaeological dig. Based on the original artefacts that were found, the later historical society reconstructed the village and the artefacts of the village, housing the originals in the museum.

While the village gives a sense of the topography of the actual fort and is set in the natural and actual landscape of the original site, everywhere the marks of years of change and progress are evident. Like the earlier view of industrial areas and the network of highways, this site is embedded in a contemporary landscape that caters to the tourist's interest in seeing "relics" of the past. The dark interiors of the Jesuit sleeping quarters and the smoky skyline of the longhouses add to the feeling of mystery and magic, but the groups of screaming schoolchildren and tourists are a part of the contemporary situation, and the tour ends at a gift shop, with many of the same artefacts as were to be found in the shrine gift shop.

The particularly Canadian landscape or topography of this pilgrimage was part of the earliest "call" or "vision" of Brébeuf and a part of the careful research of the poet in reconstructing the originary moments of call to the missionary and pilgrimage journey. The first call of Brébeuf does not give his name but describes him as "a neophyte" and recounts the vision of the pilgrimage path. In the opening lines of the poem, E. J. Pratt writes of Brebeuf's call and vow as follows:

> In contemplation saw a bleeding form
> Falling beneath the instrument of death,
> Rising under the quickening of the thongs,
> Stumbling along the Via Dolorosa.
> No play upon the fancy was this scene,
> But the Real Presence to the naked sense.
> The fingers of Brébeuf were at his breast,
> Closing and tightening on a crucifix,
> While voices spoke aloud unto his ear
> And to his heart—*per ignem et per aquam*.
> Forests and streams and trails thronged through his mind,
> The painted faces of the Iroquois,
> Nomadic bands and smoking bivouacs
> Along the shores of western inland seas,
> With forts and palisades and fiery stakes.
> —*Brébeuf and His Brethren* 94

While the initial images of the call are visions of the sacrifice or martyrdom of Christ, they are, in fact, set realistically in the Canadian setting, as Brébeuf had learned about these from explorers' journals:

> The stories of Champlain, Brûlé, Viel,
> Sagard and Le Caron reached his town –
> The stories of those northern boundaries
> Where in the winter the white pines could brush
> The Pleiades, and at the equinoxes
> Under the gold and green of the auroras
> Wild geese drove wedges through the zodiac.
> —Pratt, *Brébeuf and His Brethren* 95

It is in this vision of sacrifice in the land of the North that Brébeuf takes the vow of sacrifice that haunts the rest of the poem and pilgrimage: "*I shall be broken first before I break them*" (Pratt, *Brébeuf and His Brethren* 95).

The physical journey begins with the "three thousand miles of the Atlantic" (Pratt, *Brébeuf and His Brethren* 96), a trip that takes seven weeks. What ensues is a description of the journey that rivals the travel log/touristic details of Charles Sangster's topographic description in his long poem "The St. Lawrence and the Saguenay," an account that follows the pilgrim/missionary journey. As Pratt writes, it is "the same route Champlain and Le Caron" had followed in their explorations of the land (Pratt, *Brébeuf and His Brethren* 96). The description of the journey is worth quoting because of the trials described that are particular to the ardours of Canadian travel and because of the sense it conveys of the first Canadian pilgrim trail over land and water—an aspect of the journey perhaps unique to the Canadian pilgrim experience:

> Through steep gorges where the river narrowed,
> Through calmer waters where the river widened,
> Skirting the island of the Allumettes,
> Thence to the Mattawa through lakes that led
> To the blue waters of the Nipissing,
> And then southward a hundred tortuous miles
> Down the French River to the Huron shore.
> —Pratt, *Brébeuf and His Brethren* 98

This first part of the journey gives the most basic of topographical details: the width of the river, the calmness of the water, the color of the water, the names of the lakes, the length of the journey, and the arrival at the destination. Moreover, these details are complete with the beautiful native names of the rivers, an aspect of the poetic language that makes this charter pilgrimage distinctively Canadian. The lines that follow give a sense of the torture involved in this journey for Brébeuf as well as from the mental and actual reliving of the pilgrimage in the days that follow:

> The record of that trip was for Brébeuf
> A memory several times to be re-lived;
> Of rocks and cataracts and portages,
> Of feet cut by the river stones, of mud
> And stench, of boulders, logs and tangled growths,
> Of summer heat that made him long for night,
> And when he struck his bed of rock—mosquitoes
> That made him doubt if dawn would ever break.
> —Pratt, *Brébeuf and His Brethren* 98

Again following the description of what he endured, readers are given a realistic physical description of the land and place names, beginning with Georgian Bay and recounting the number of days it took, the number of miles, description of the landscape, and finally the home they built and the length of time they lived there: "'Twas thirty days to Georgian Bay, then south / One hundred miles threading the labyrinth / Of islands till he reached the western shore / That flanked the Bay of Penetanguishene" (Pratt, *Brébeuf and His Brethren* 98), the journey concluding with "The course of a small stream [reaching] Toanché, / Where for three years he was to make his home" (Pratt, *Brébeuf and His Brethren* 98). In some ways the ardours of this first physical journey from the comforts of the earthly home in France to the wilderness of Canada is only a glimpse or a foretaste of the journey that is to follow. Like Christ's temptation in the desert, the real testing would come in the walk of the cross and the death of the cross, and so too for Brébeuf this journey was only the first trial of many that would follow, the first taste of the cup of suffering from which he freely drank in the years that followed.

The next pilgrimage journey in some ways repeats the earlier journey "eight years before" (Pratt, *Brébeuf and His Brethren* 104). However, by 1634 "the native mood / [w]as hostile" (Pratt, *Brébeuf and His Brethren* 104). First Davost, "robbed of his books," is deserted "at the Island of the Allumettes," and then the others are one by one put ashore and deserted (Pratt, *Brébeuf and His Brethren* 104). The priests continue their journey on foot, "all in turn, / tattered, wasted, with feet / Bleeding—broken though not in will, rejoined / The forest shores of the Fresh Water Sea" (Pratt, *Brébeuf and His Brethren* 104), and they eventually make their way, guided by the "sight of smoke," to "[t]he village of Ihonatiria" (Pratt, *Brébeuf and His Brethren* 104).

In both the "1626" and the "1634" sections, following the Canadian pilgrimage journey, are agriculturally oriented passages, describing the work of the priests on the land and employing the metaphor of farming for the tilling and harvesting of native souls. The intimate connection between the conquest of land and souls and the sum of the imperial project is never more apparent, although the precedent for this metaphor is found in the writings of St. Paul, previously discussed in the theological work of the poet. Like Paul, Pratt uses agriculture as a way to describe the missionary practices of the Jesuits with the Huron tribe: "From the pursuit of agriculture he took the figure of sowing and reaping, of germination and increase" (Pratt, *Brébeuf and His Brethren* 33). In the section entitled "1626" the poet writes: "'Twas ploughing only—for eight years would pass / Before even the blades appeared" (Pratt, *Brébeuf and His Brethren* 98). The metaphor is made more explicit with clear colonial implications in the "1634" section:

> A year's success flattered the priestly hope
> That on this central field seed would be sown
> On which the yield would be the Huron nation
> Baptized and dedicated to the Faith;
> And that a richer harvest would be gleaned
> Of duskier grain from the same seed on more
> Forbidding ground.
>
> —Pratt, *Brébeuf and His Brethren* 104-5

Here, there is no question that the subject is the Native of a "duskier grain."

The next phase of colonization and the "pilgrim" conquest of the Jesuits is the building of a "mission house" and the establishment of permanent dwelling among the Huron people. Utilizing the labour of the natives, "The Fathers built their mission house—the frame / Of young elm-poles set solidly in the earth; / Their supple tops bent, lashed and braced to form / The arched roof overlaid with cedar-bark" (Pratt, *Brébeuf and His Brethren* 105). Although the Fathers use the materials native to the land, everywhere the comparison is made to the cathedrals and dwelling places in France. Quoting from *The Jesuit Relations*, Pratt notes, "No Louvre or palace is this cabin," and the comparison continues to describe the Native-style equivalents to the rooms and chapels of France. The second mission of St. Joseph is described in garrison language:

> The place was fortified, ramparts were strengthened,
> And towers of heavy posts set at the angles.
> And in the following year the artisans
> And labourers from Quebec and Du Peron,
> Using broad-axe and whipsaw built a church,
> The first one in the whole Huronian venture
> To be of wood. Close to their lodge.
>
> —Pratt, *Brébeuf and His Brethren* 116

The chapel in the fortified town is called "their Rheims Cathedral," again making explicit the transposition and imposition of European and French values and culture to the Native soil.

The pinnacle of French temporal and spiritual achievement is the building of a French-fortified city described in the poem as "THE FOUNDING OF FORT SAINTE MARIE," destined to be a place where "[t]he priests with their attendants might pursue / Their culture, gather strength from their devotions, / Map out the territory, plot the routes, / Collate their weekly notes and write their letters" (Pratt, *Brébeuf and His Brethren* 118). Both a process of colonization and a physical mapping of the territories covered in their missionary journeys takes place within the walls of the fort. This record becomes important in later anthropological reconstruction and in the poetic mapping of the topography of the journeys, forts, and sacred sites that were constructed during the days of Jesuit pilgrimage and missionary activity. The fort, while constructed as a religious center for the Jesuits, also "received approval from Quebec, / Was ratified by Richelieu who saw / Commerce and exploration pushing west, / Fulfilling the long vision of Champlain— / '*Greater New France beyond the inland seas*'" (Pratt, *Brébeuf and His Brethren* 119). In Fort Sainte Marie the vision and call of the explorer, the economic demands of the imperial power, and the establishment of a central sacred site are all combined in the garrisoned Fort nestled in the Canadian landscape:

> The fort was built, two hundred feet by ninety,
> Upon the right bank of the River Wye:
> Its north and eastern sides of masonry,
> Its south and west of palisades,
> And skirted by a moat, ran parallel
> To stream and lake. Square bastions at the corners,
> Watch-towers with magazines and sleeping posts,
> Commanded forest edges and canoes
> That furtively came up the Matchedash,
> And on each bastion was placed a cross.
> —Pratt, *Brébeuf and His Brethren* 119

The fort's construction is completed with the sacred approval of the symbol of Christ's death and suffering and the power of the Church in the new world. This section ends with "a census of the Huron nation; / Some thirty villages—twelve thousand persons. / Nor was this all: the horizon opened out / On larger fields. To south and west were spread / The unknown tribes—the Petuns and the Neutrals" (Pratt, *Brébeuf and His Brethren* 120). Again these verses reinforce the idea of the "Huron nation" and "the horizon" beyond this nation as "fields" for exploration, conquest, and cultivation, employing the agricultural metaphor to both the known and unknown territories. The estimates of the numbers of Hurons by the Jesuits and those quoted here by Pratt ("thirty villages—twelve thousand persons") continue to be used in the anthropological studies of the Wendat nation and appear to be fairly accurate estimates for that region and time.[5]

The further journeys into the interior of the land, away from Georgian Bay and into the bleak Canadian winter landscape, are described in "THE MISSION OF THE PETUNS AND NEUTRALS," dating 1640-1641. The poet writes, "In late November Jogues and Garnier / Set out on snow-obliterated trails / Towards the Blue Hills south of Nottawasaga, / A thirty mile journey through a forest / Without a guide" (Pratt, *Brébeuf and His Brethren* 120). Without trails or guide the difficulties of the journey, including "swamps with fallen logs" and "Tangles of tamarack and juniper," all contribute to the bleakness of the journey as well as the characteristic difficulty of a pilgrimage. The description ceases to be that of the explorer and becomes more characteristic of the wanderer in the desert of the Canadian winter: "Ever in hope their tread was towards the south" (Pratt, *Brébeuf and His Brethren* 120). Their search is described as "hopeless," but they repeatedly give thanks to God for the cathedrals of "a fir grove" where, following prayer, they "lay down and slept" (Pratt, *Brébeuf and His Brethren* 120). These verses at the same time echo the description of Christ and his disciples praying on the night before his betrayal, complete with the outdoor/wild garden and the eventual exhausted sleep of the disciples, and they allude to the eventual betrayal and martyrdom of Brébeuf. At the same time, Pratt also invokes the Hebrew tradition of pilgrimage. Just as the Israelites wandered through the desert, in hopes of finding the Promised Land, with their only guide by night the pillar of fire, the priests are likewise guided by their hope and the "smoke" of the Indian village fires. However, by this point in the Jesuit missionary activities, finding the Indian villages is only the signal of further suffering. The Jesuits became associated with plague and death, and they are "driven from town to town with all doors barred" (Pratt, *Brébeuf and His Brethren* 121). The wanderings and suffering of Jogues and Garnier are only a prelude to the "bleak outlook" that was to await Brébeuf also in his "November tramp" (Pratt, *Brébeuf and His Brethren* 121). Brébeuf spends four months tramping through the forest, blood mixing with the snow, led

> Along an incandescent avenue
> The visions trembled, tender, placid, pure,
> More beautiful than the doorway of Rheims
> And sweeter than the Galilean fields.
> For what was hunger and the burn of wounds
> In those assuaging, healing moments when
> The clearing mists revealed the face of Mary
> And the lips of Jesus breathing benedictions?
> —Pratt, *Brébeuf and His Brethren* 121

The barren winter snows then mix with the blood of suffering, and on this bleak landscape appear the visions of divine mercy and blessing possible only in the extremes of suffering and privation. Brébeuf's final vision in this section as he comes "limping through the postern of the fort" (Pratt, *Brébeuf and His Brethren* 124) is of "a moving cross," which he writes of in his letters as "huge enough to crucify us all" (Pratt, *Brébeuf and His Brethren* 124).

The poet's vision and Brébeuf's vision end with the image of the cross, an image which stands in Catholic and Christian iconography for ultimate sacrifice and ultimate love. However, the tourist or pilgrim of today cannot help but see that the vision of these earliest Canadian pilgrims, the construction of the site, and the text of *Brébeuf and His Brethren* are riddled with problems of representation, empire, and, indeed, with the problems of constructing a nationalistic memorial for a movement that was inspired by faith but that resulted in the death of the martyrs and colonial expansion. In fact, at the shrine today, the monument that follows the walk through Brébeuf's Prayer Garden, the site of his visions of the cross and sacrifice, is a single cross made of field rocks and intended to represent the sacrifice of the Huron nation. Gazing at the rocks lumped together as a Catholic memorial of the Hurons' sacrifice, it becomes necessary to look at it and the Catholic narrative of Christian sacrifice in terms that also include postcolonial questioning of representation.

Notes

[1] Vincent Sharman in the Pratt issue of *Canadian Literature* writes that, "For Pratt, what men must understand is that their salvation lies in themselves, not in Nature, God, systems or in ignorant pride in machines. To maintain life should be the end of men's actions, the accomplishment of which, in times of conflict, is dependent on defiance, determination and Reason under the control of the heart. But illusions persist: men kill men, die for ideals which embrace death and delude themselves with hopeful prayers addressed to the 'unhearing ears of God.' Imperfect men must make direct their feelings for other men for the sake of life. For life is, finally, all that men have, and only men can care at all whether men live or die" (qtd. in Pitt, *E. J. Pratt: Critical Views on Canadian Writers: E.J. Pratt* 151). The humanistic readings of Pratt and his poetry may, in fact, come from his own reading of the character of the Jesuits and their mission. Pratt writes that "in the course of their religious endeavours they never ignored the humane and social side of their ministrations. They strove to reduce disease in the villages, to improve sanitation and hygiene, to mitigate, if they could not abolish, the torture of captured enemies. They taught new methods of cultivation" (Gingell, *Collected Works* xxix). Pratt concludes that his role is "to humanize, as far as possible, the priest" (Gingell, *Collected Works* xxix).

The confusion surrounding Pratt is further heightened when Sandra Djwa first misrepresents Pratt as having been ordained as a minister in the United Church when, in fact, he served as a minister in the Methodist church; she then goes on to attribute *Brébeuf and His Brethren* to an apologetic impulse on the part of the poet to his father and as further evidence of his "crisis of faith." Djwa writes, "[s]cattered comments from those who knew him and the evidence of the unpublished *Clay*, written just as he was concluding his doctorate (on Pauline eschatology) suggest that Pratt suffered a crisis of faith and came to the conclusion that he was not suited for the religious life. We might speculate that part of the appeal of the Brébeuf narrative may have been that it was the account of a man who did continue in the religious life; in Pratt's *Brébeuf* the focus is very often upon motivation. Furthermore, the poem is dedicated to Pratt's father who was for many years a Methodist minister in Newfoundland. In this context, the poem may be seen not only as an exploration of the religious experience but also, perhaps, as Pratt's own apologia to the father whose example he could not follow" (Djwa 93).

[2] Hunt claims that critics writing about this poem do not understand Christian belief and that understanding of this poem "depends on response to the whole of the Christian tradition, both as it is seminally embodied in the *New Testament*, and as it may be apprehended in the religious history of the past two thousand years" (70). Indeed, Hunt actually drops the critical debate as to the religious orientation of the poet and takes on the religious orientation of the critics suggesting that their beliefs lead to false readings.

[3] In 1948 archaeologist Wilfrid Jury headed up a group of archaeologists funded by the University of Western Ontario. E. J. Pratt, a friend and confidant of Wilfrid Jury, visited the site and consulted Jury about various topographical and anthropological issues in his research for the writing of *Brébeuf and His Brethren.*

[4] The original citation for this piece is Massimo Centini, "*La Vie Alpine Fra Storia e Mito: Appunti per una Ricerca*," *Lungo le Vie Della Fede* (Piazzola sul Brenta: Papergraf, 1999), 49. It appears, translated into English by Luigi Tomasi, in William Swatos and Luigi Tomasi, *From Medieval Pilgrimage to Religious Tourism.*

[5] For a more detailed discussion of the various estimates of numbers and territories of the Hurons and the various explorers, anthropologists, and sociologists to make these estimates see Bruce G. Trigger's *The Huron Farmers of the North.*

Works Cited

Augustine, Saint, Bishop of Hippo. *The Confessions of Saint Augustine*. Trans. Edward B. Pusey. New York: Random House, 1949.

Coleman, Simon and John Elsner. *Pilgrimage: Past and Present in the World Religions.* Cambridge: Harvard UP, 1995.

Djwa, Sandra. *E. J. Pratt: The Evolutionary Vision*. Montreal: McGill-Queen's UP, 1974.

Hunt, Peter. "E. J. Pratt's *Brébeuf and His Brethren*: The Critics and the Sources." *The E. J. Pratt Symposium. Reappraisals of Canadian Writers*. Ed. Glenn Clever. Ottawa, Can.: U of Ottawa Press, 1977. 69-89.

Gingell, Susan, ed. *The Collected Works of E. J. Pratt: E. J. Pratt on His Life and Poetry.* Toronto: U Toronto P, 1983.

—. *E. J. Pratt: Pursuits Amateur and Academic: The Selected Prose of E. J. Pratt.* Toronto: U Toronto P, 1995.

McAuliffe, Angela T. *Between the Temple and the Cave: The Religious Dimensions of the Poetry of E. J. Pratt*. Montreal & Kingston, Can.: McGill-Queen's UP, 2000.

Mealing, S. R., ed. *The Jesuit Relations and Allied Documents: A Selection.* Toronto: McClelland and Stewart, 1963.

Morinis, Alan, ed. *Sacred Journeys: The Anthropology of Pilgrimage*. London, Can.: Greenwood, 1992.

Pitt, David G. *E. J. Pratt. Critical Views on Canadian Writers.* Toronto: Ryerson Press, 1969.

—. *E. J. Pratt: The Truant Years, 1882-1927*. Toronto: U Toronto P, 1984.

Pratt, E[dwin]. J[ohn]. *Brébeuf and His Brethren.* Toronto: Macmillan Co. of Canada Ltd., 1940.

Preston, James J. "Spiritual Magnetism: An Organizing Principle for the Study of Pilgrimage." *Sacred Journeys: The Anthropology of Pilgrimage.* Ed. Alan Morinis. Toronto: McClelland and Stewart, 1963. 31-46.

Sangster, Charles. "The St. Lawrence and the Saguenay." Ed. D. M. R. Bentley. *Early Long Poems on Canada.* London, Can.: Canadian Poetry Press, 1993. 401-450.

Swatos, William H. and Tomasi, Luigi, eds. *From Medieval Pilgrimage to Religious Tourism: The Social and Cultural Economics of Piety.* London: Praeger, 2002.

Trigger, Bruce G. *The Huron Farmers of the North.* Toronto: Holt, Rinehart and Winston, 1969.

Turner, Victor and Edith Turner. *Image and Pilgrimage in Christian Culture.* New York: Columbia UP, 1978.

Wilson, Milton. *E. J. Pratt.* Toronto and Montreal: McClelland and Stewart Limited, 1969.

Chapter Six

Maintaining a Wide Margin: The Boat as House in Beatrice Grimshaw's Travel Writing

Clare McCotter

This paper focuses on Beatrice Grimshaw's second travelogue, *In the Strange South Seas* (1907). Demonstrating a degree of ambivalence, flexibility and openness *vis-à-vis* class and race, this text differs noticeably from her other travel writing and also from much of her fiction. It must be said from the outset, however, that this volume is concerned with the eastern Pacific. It is therefore possible that Grimshaw's engagement with race simply reflects colonial stereotypes which tended to favor Polynesians at the expense of their Oceanic neighbors. Alternatively, Susan Gardner suggests that the marked ambiguity of the book may result from the nature of Grimshaw's commission (107-8).[1] While these factors are of undoubted significance to any consideration of narrative voice in *In the Strange South Seas*, I would like to postulate a third variable: the influence of the Pacific itself and the mode of travel which Grimshaw enjoyed during those months that she toured the islands.[2] Describing a world of seascapes and boat journeys, *In the Strange South Seas* is the most nautical of Grimshaw's travel books and the one in which Grimshaw the traveler appears to be most content. And perhaps she was, for, if travel is an exploration of both the infinite and the finite, the unfenced and the fenced, then the months that Grimshaw spent on the little trading schooner the *Duchess* offered an almost perfect synthesis of the two. This colonial tourist could experience the vastness of the Pacific from the bounded space of the boat.

On a physical level, the boat is a bounded space, one which this paper, drawing on the work of Roland Barthes and Gaston Bachelard, argues is, in the first instance, a home. Enclosed and surrounded by the amniotic sea, the boat in many ways replicates the first home—the mother/womb/tomb. It incorporates, as we shall see, the semiotic and the symbolic, life and death, as indeed does the uterus itself. For the maternal is not a pre-symbolic site; our history, individual and collective, is em*bodied*. Influencing and being influenced by the journey, it travels with us. Home is always present in the away. What it means in the elsewhere will vary greatly. No two homes, regardless of whether the mother/first home or the first house, will be inhabited in the same way. The home is a site of contradictions: supposedly a private sphere, it is inescapably informed by the public. A putative site of rest and recuperation, for some it is a place of subversion, counter-culture, political action, the only place from which they can plan and dream. Despite strenuous efforts to reinforce lines of demarcation, borders and margins, the public is always ineluctably present in the private. This work examines the late nineteenth-century preoccupation with margins and the boundaries. It posits this concern as a futile attempt to cast off the abject, that which can never be cast off. The *out* is always already *in*. It is argued in this paper that Cloona House, the first house that Grimshaw inhabited, the marker of her family's status and its demise, a place of security and its absence, a source of rootedness and disconnection, of stasis and movement, influenced how she inhabited the small trading schooner, the home in motion, from which she viewed the blue infinitude of the Pacific.

The tropic sea was many things to Grimshaw, but perhaps more than anything else it signalled color, color ranging from changeless blue to luminous plains of beautiful opalescence. In *In the Strange South Seas* Grimshaw states:

> Emerald and jade and sapphire—yes, one expects these, in the hues of tropic seas. But when it comes to whole tracts of glancing heliotrope and hyacinth, shot with unnameable shades of melted turquoise and silver, and all a-quiver with pulsations of flashing greens, for which there is no name in any language under the pallid northern or burning southern sun—then, the thing becomes indescribable, and one can only say: "There is something in that little corner of earth beyond the touch of words [.] (2)

In using the word "indescribable," Grimshaw indicates that part of the range of colors that make up the Pacific lie beyond language; they lie "beyond the touch of words" (137). Representation of this ocean can only ever be partial. Grimshaw's Pacific is a "magical sea" (138). Playful and chimerical, it undermines ocular authority: "The raised appearance of the lagoon is one of the strangest things I have yet seen, though it is merely an optical delusion, created by contrast in colour" (127). During a reefing party, Grimshaw, to the amusement of her friends, also discovers that the "pinky-violet" coral which she manages to detach and bring to the surface is "liver-coloured" (100) once out of the water. But this ludic quality resides only on the surface or in the shallows; the deep harbors myriad dangers.

> Under water among the coral reefs! It sounds romantic, but it was not pleasant. Five feet beneath the surface, the light was as clear as day, and one could see all about one, far too much, for the things that were visible were disquieting. (201)

Although a strong swimmer, Grimshaw expresses intense discomfort and fear of swimming below the surface.[3] While always conscious of sharks, her fear of the deep is largely restricted to underwater activity. In *In the Strange South Seas,* while discussing a bathing trip undertaken with some island girls from Niué, Grimshaw describes an unpleasant underwater experience; she encounters what she afterwards thinks may have been a "big devil fish" (202). The incident leaves her very shaken, but, rather than swimming for the shore, she simply decides to keep her head above sea level: "And on the surface I stayed, for the rest of the swim" (201). For Grimshaw the ocean is most threatening when one is submerged in it; she appears to believe that she is in less danger if she can see the sky. During her stay on Tonga, for example, she spends many hours swimming alone at night, surrendering herself to the rhythms of the ocean, with her gaze focused on the surface swell and the stars above:

> the dark shining water bearing one to and fro with the swell from the reef, the land growing further and further away [...] Willingly indeed one would have passed the whole night out there, swimming, and floating in a warm dark sea of stars—stars above stars below—if nature had not given out after an hour or two, and demanded a return to the solid earth. (266)

Grimshaw delights in the fusion of air and sea. Relaxed on the surface of the water where she can see the sky, her fear of what lurks beneath, while not extinguished, is certainly diminished.

Grimshaw's fear of the deep, her fear of sharks, her fear of being consumed are all very real fears; it is therefore all the more remarkable that she decided to confront this terror in the manner that she did: donning a cumbersome deep sea suit and diving solo to a depth of thirty feet in the notorious Torres straits. She describes this incident in her third travelogue, *The New New Guinea* (1910):

> You look ahead through the darkling water for the swoop and rush and horrible scythe-shaped tail of the monster that you fear, but there is no sign of it [...] Still—you have been down some minutes now, and honour is amply satisfied. It would be very pleasant to see the light of day again[.] (219)

Contemplating the nature of her fear prior to the dive, Grimshaw claims:

> The sober truth, I think, is that a woman always is afraid of doing dangerous things. Generally she lies about it, partly through conceit, and largely because she is curious and does not mind being horribly afraid if you will give her what she

> wants. But the truth is as I have said. The cold courage of the male—the Nelson courage that "never saw fear"—is not in any woman who ever was born. (216-7)

In an extremely ambiguous statement about gender, the detached and passionless mental state that Grimshaw attributes to Nelson seems much closer to psychopathy than bravery. Courage cannot exist without fear, but, by highlighting the latter, Grimshaw is simultaneously italicizing the former. There is no doubt that her courage/fear is acute; prior to descent, anxiety is palpable, fear not only of the dimension that she is entering, but also of departure from the one that she is in. Commenting on the dive, Gaston Bachelard states:

> we come to a point where we recognise in this space-substance, a one-dimensional space. One substance, one dimension. And we are so remote from the earth and life on earth, that this dimension of water bears the mark of limitlessness. (205)

Grimshaw does not experience this space-substance as liberating, something Bachelard's use of the signifier "limitlessness" tends to suggest; once on the sea bed she soon begins to long for the "light of day" and is eternally grateful for "the sweetness of that first rush of warm tropic air" (219). The one dimension of this absolute element unnerves Grimshaw. For her a sense of limitlessness is most fully realized when occupying the liminal position of partial submersion, body moving in both air and water, a position which replicates that occupied by the boat.

In his ruminations on the boat, Roland Barthes, while recognizing that it "may well be a symbol for departure" goes on to add that it is:

> at a deeper level, the emblem of closure. An inclination for ships always means the joy of perfectly enclosing oneself, and having at hand the greatest possible number of objects, and having at one's disposal an absolutely finite space. To like ships is first and foremost to like a house, a superlative one[.] (66)

Decisively bounded the boat is house, the ultimate one, the one that not only encloses but also creates, on a physical level, the widest possible sterile zone between its inhabitants and potential sources of contagion. While it could be argued that islands perform the same function, from a human perspective they may not only be uninhabited but also uninhabitable. Boats imply a human presence, a place of habitation; they suggest a space that is emphatically bounded. Anne McClintock argues that during the Victorian period a desire for boundaries and definite lines of demarcation became an increasingly important aspect of middle-class society:

> A characteristic feature of the Victorian middle class was its peculiarly intense preoccupation with rigid boundaries. In imperial fiction and commodity kitsch, boundary objects and liminal scenes recur ritualistically. As colonials traveled back and forth across the thresholds of their known world, crisis and boundary confusion were warded off and contained by fetishes, absolution rituals and liminal scenes. Soap and cleaning rituals became central to the demarcation of body boundaries and the policing of social hierarchies. (33)

The latter was of crucial importance not only within a colonial context but also in the metropolitan center. As urbanization accelerated in the nineteenth century, the classes were living in closer proximity to each other, something which could explain the increased focus on borders and boundaries. While McClintock recognizes that "[c]leansing and boundary rituals are integral to most cultures," she goes on to add that what characterized Victorian cleaning rituals was not only their prevalence but also "their peculiarly intense relation to money" (33). With the commercial manufacture of soap emerging as an important industry in the nineteenth century, cleaning rituals became commoditized and objectified in the sense that certain boundary markers, such as doors, doorknockers, doorsteps, were, at times, the focus of acute attention (McClintock 208). Describing house work as a "semiotics of boundary maintenance," McClintock in her discussion of the middle-class Victorian home states:

> Servants spent much of their time cleaning boundary objects—doorknobs, windowsills, steps, pathways, flagstones, curtains and banisters, not because these objects were especially dirty, but because scrubbing and polishing them ritually maintained the boundaries between private and public and gave these objects exhibition value as class markers. (170)

The constant polishing of doorknobs and the scrubbing of steps was an attempt to maintain the integrity of the increasingly insular and—with the demise of cottage industries and the development of the factory system—de-industrialized home by creating a margin around it from which the abject was supposedly excluded. Describing the abject, Julia Kristeva states that "it is something rejected from which one does not part" (*Powers* 4). Producing unease or even nausea, the abject is that which we conceptualize as dirt and contagion, that which must be cast off but which from which distance can never be maintained. Kristeva writes that "It is thus not lack of cleanliness or health that causes abjection but what disturbs identity, system, order" (4). "Above all ambiguity" (9), the abject—in its most obvious manifestation "*corporeal waste*, menstrual blood and excrement, or everything that is assimilated to them, from nail-parings to decay"—is that which threatens boundaries, threatens the dichotomy between inside and outside (70). The cleaning of street flags and the scrubbing of doorsteps in the nineteenth century was an attempt to maintain a margin or buffer zone between the *in* and the *out*.

Surrounded by its sea-moat, no other habitation more decisively suggests a space of demarcation than the boat. In the second half of the nineteenth century, the vessel that was increasingly being constructed as a locus of insular, islanded, frequently luxurious domesticity was the yacht.[4] Prior to the Prince of Wales's acquisition of the *Britannia* in 1893, the best-known English yacht was probably Thomas Brassey's *Sunbeam*, and one of the most discussed journeys was the 37,000 mile world cruise which the Brasseys, their family, and extensive crew undertook in 1876-7 and which Annie Brassey documented in *A Voyage In The Sunbeam* (1879). The *Sunbeam* was the family's home on the ocean wave, and like all domestic sites it incorporated the public. Much of the Brasseys' journey took place within a colonial context; it was the spread of European imperialism that made their trip possible. This fusion of public and private is reflected in the interior of the *Sunbeam*: it is a home that houses an imperial museum. Annie Brassey shops, trades, and barters incessantly. The vessel contains innumerable and disparate collections—birds, animals, botanical specimens, shells, handicrafts, and clothes. The *Sunbeam*'s appetite for the products of the colonized world is voracious and insatiable. Indeed it could well be its ability to house collections, thus facilitating colonial trade (or plunder), that led to the popularity of long-distance cruising during the age of high imperialism. It was not enough to have an empire; empire had to be displayed. On board the yacht the Other could be viewed from a safe distance, left behind on the shore, kept away from one's home. Empire could be rendered visible; it could be translated into a spectacle. Domesticity, colonial trade, and the museumization of other cultures are fused within the space of the yacht, a space invariably gendered feminine. As McClintock observes "Sailors bound wooden female figures to their ships" prows and baptized their ships—as exemplary threshold objects—with their female names" (24). By using female names to suggest a site of bounded domesticity sailors were attempting to establish the boat's *insideness*, attempting to cement a clear line of demarcation between the known and the unknown, the inside and the out.

However, boundary markers do not stop here. On the boat itself there are degrees of *insideness*. Possibly the most obvious nautical boundary marker is the deck. Open to the elements, the deck covers the more private, uterine-like space that lies beneath enclosed within a world of fluidity. A very definite threshold position, the deck is the boat's doorstep, and on all "good" vessels it was as well scrubbed as the step of any middle-class Victorian home. Discipline on the *Duchess*, the trading schooner on which Grimshaw traveled across huge swathes of the Pacific, was, however, more relaxed than that found on board most English yachts of the period. She states "There is no "let-her-slide" spirit in the whole world to compare with that which blossoms spontaneously on the sun-white decks of a Pacific schooner (*In the Strange South Seas* 119-20). Grimshaw describes the *Duchess* as "my home" (119), which it was for those four months that she spent on board. Grimshaw was clearly attracted by boats: after her arrival in Papua she had three double canoes strapped together and a home constructed upon them. Grimshaw had been the guest of Papua's colonial Governor J. H. P. Murray at Government House. She had also stayed at "the 'Top Pub', one of Port Moresby's two" (Laracy 160), but she left these addresses, preferring instead her canoes moored in the sea, of which she writes, "I loved that house until it became the meeting place for crocodiles who lived in the surrounding shallows and bellowed like bulls at night" ("How I Found Adventure" 3).

Throughout her life Grimshaw would spend time on boats, traveling on luxury liners, on a missionary launch in Papua, and of course as Murray's guest on Papua's government launch *Merrie England*. The latter was an orderly boat with a beautiful interior, and yet the voice that emerges from the *Duchess* seems happier, more relaxed, less in need of the seemingly well-organized world of colonial plantations. This is not to suggest that order did not exist on the *Duchess*. There is still a wide margin between sea and land, and the door to Grimshaw's cabin is a decisive boundary marker. Nevertheless the order that Grimshaw experiences on the *Duchess* is different from that to which she is accustomed; it is a scuffed, sometimes threadbare type of order that facilitates a degree of interracial and, in particular, interclass intimacy. Describing breakfast on the schooner for herself and the white members of the crew, Grimshaw states:

> Clawing like a parrot, the passenger reaches the cabin, and finds the bare-armed, barefooted mates and the captain engaged on the inevitable "tin" and biscuits. There is no tea this morning, because the cockroaches have managed to get in and flavour the brew[.] (*In the Strange South Seas* 220)

Grimshaw seems to spend a good deal of time interacting with these men in a way that does not suggest concern about class distinctions: "Lying on the poop, like seals on sand, the little knot of passengers, captain, and mate, 'yarned' for hour after hour—strange, wild tales of frontier life in new lands" (156-7). The image of the seals suggests a group of people who are totally relaxed in each other's company, while also indicating close physical proximity.

Abandoning steam for sail, it is during this lengthy voyage around the Pacific on the little schooner that Grimshaw appears to be at the mercy of the elements more than at any other time in her travels. The Pacific demands flexibility. Unlike a tract of forest put under the planter's axe, it cannot be controlled. This is a seascape that is in motion and one that can clearly talk back. When the captain of the trading schooner on which Grimshaw is traveling attempts to explore and chart Beveridge Reef, heavy squalls upend his boat, almost resulting in loss of life. Concluding her description of the incident Grimshaw states, "And so we left the reef in the growing dusk, and no man has to this day disturbed the virgin surface of its stormy little lagoon with profanely invading oar" (*In the Strange South Seas* 177). This is a victory to the ocean, and Grimshaw is uncomplaining. Entirely dependent on the wind, timetables for this trip have to be extremely elastic. The hard-riding equestrienne of *From Fiji to the Cannibal Islands* (1907), who harried her guides, pressing them on to reach the appointed destination each evening, is gone. A more relaxed narrator emerges *In the Strange South Seas*. Although the mindscape that she projects is not free from barriers, it certainly appears less trammelled, less encumbered, less rigid than in her other travelogues. Grimshaw's second travelogue, *In the Strange South Seas*, exhibits a degree of openness, a widening of horizons that is not as evident in her other non-fiction. Those seascapes which surrounded her for months on end during the voyages described in this volume may have quietly eroded a few barriers, perhaps none more important than those between the races.

In the following quotation from *In the Strange South Seas* Grimshaw represents indigenous sailors in predictably stereotypical terms:

> Native crews are the rule in the South Seas, and native crews make work for everyone including themselves. Absolutely fearless is the Kanaka, active as a monkey aloft, good natured and jolly to the last degree, but perfectly unreliable in any matter requiring an once of thought or a pennyworth of discretion[.] (217-8)

But Grimshaw also moves beyond this stance. Presented in the above *en masse*, later in the text the crew are individualized: "Tapitua, who is a great dandy, puts two gold earrings in one ear, and fastens a wreath of cock's feathers about his hat. Koddi (christened George) gets into a thick blue woollen jersey […] Ta puts on three different singlets—a pink, a blue, and a yellow" (222). And so it goes on until all are named and their attire described. While it could be argued that Grimshaw is merely poking fun at the men's fashion sense, I do not think that this is the case. She concludes this passage by saying "Truly we are a gay party, by the time every one is ready to land" (222). The viewing *I* is translated into a *we*; Grimshaw is not disembarking as an individual but as part of a group, a collective including black and white. Although fleeting, a moment of communitas has been achieved within the liminal space of the *Duchess*.

Grimshaw's colonial encounters in *In the Strange South Seas* embody a much greater degree of openness and acceptance. As she shares accommodation with islanders, as she goes on swimming and fishing trips with them, some of these relationships start to exhibit a degree of intimacy. One of numerous examples takes place on the island of Atiu, where Grimshaw and the local women spend some time in a hairdressing session. Commenting on this activity Grimshaw states:

> We had a good deal of feminine talk among ourselves, before the men came out again: the fact that I did not know anything of the language, save perhaps half a dozen words, was no bar to a certain amount of thought-interchange. How was it done? Signs, for the most part: scraps, guesses, hints, stray native words made to do double and treble duty. Could I have talked to the husbands and brothers of the women in the same way? No, certainly not. (152)

Temporary, makeshift and partial, this radiantly evanescent system of signification, lying beyond the space of stale phallogocentric speech, is a body language. It is, according to Grimshaw, a type of communication which men can not appreciate: “Women, who have talked the ‘sign language’ to each other, many and many a time, over the innocent thick heads of their unsuspecting better-halves, friends or brothers, will never doubt it” (152). Grimshaw goes on to add “We are not as clever as men—let the equality brigade shriek if they like, ‘it’s as true as turnips is, as true as taxes’—but neither are we as stupid” (152). This is another markedly ambiguous statement about gender. Grimshaw asserts that women are not as intelligent as men immediately after referring to the male center of learning as “innocent” and “thick.” It is a remark that must be read within its literary context, sitting as it does amid a body of travel writing in which a female author offers endless advice to men on subjects such as imperial politics, agriculture, horticulture, economics, defence, travel, emigration, and architecture.

Grimshaw’s engagement with gender is complex and contradictory. She dismisses contemporary feminists as the “equality brigade,” while leading a life that eschewed many of the norms governing what was considered appropriate female behavior at that time. Grimshaw constructed a life in the South Seas that provided her with a considerable degree of freedom, a life surrounded by what she, quoting Thoreau, referred to as “a broad margin” (qtd. in “Where the Read Gods Call” 21). As a new arrival in Oceania, recently released from the routine of nine to five, Grimshaw’s first experience of this less rigorously fenced existence would have been her time on board the *Duchess*. Those restrictions that she experienced elsewhere, particularly in that much earlier home, were lessened to a considerable extent. Reminiscing in the *Blue Book* on her home in Belfast Grimshaw reflects:

> I was taught to ride and play games. I was taught to behave. To write notes for Mamma. To do the flowers. To be polite but not too polite, to Young Gentlemen. To accept flowers, sweets and books from then, but no more. To rise swiftly with

> the rest of the six daughters and sons when Papa came into the breakfast-room, to kiss him ceremoniously, and rush to wait upon him. He liked it, and we liked it. (1)

While Grimshaw ends on a positive note, there seems to be much here with which she was less than enamored: 19 College Gardens was a home in which she did not stay any longer than was necessary:

> But I was the Revolting Daughter—as they called them then. I bought a bicycle, with difficulty. I rode it unchaperoned, mile and miles beyond the limits possible to the soberly trotting horses. The world opened up before me. And as soon as my twenty-first birthday dawned, I went away from home, to see what the world might give to daughters who revolted. (1)

Grimshaw would undoubtedly have appreciated George Sand's *cri de coeur* "What is more beautiful than a road" (qtd. in Bachelard 11). As a young equestrienne at Cloona House and later as an enthusiastic cyclist, she craved movement, and it was a persistent driving force throughout her long life. College Gardens and all the subsequent homes that she either owned or rented, even the "Dream Houses" described in *Isles Of Adventure* (1930), were places to be left. Yet, in a letter written to an Australian friend Margaret Windeyer in 1912, Grimshaw states:

> I was very glad to hear that you are well and that your home affairs are happy. You don't know how different life looks when the home breaks up and you warm yourself henceforth by other folk's fires. Of course yours never may; there may always be some of your people left in the old place. I hope there will be. (qtd. in Laracy 155)

Susan Gardner has pointed out that, when Grimshaw died in St Vincent's Hospital at Bathurst, one of very few personal effects was a photograph of Cloona House. She had carried this image of her family's country home around with her all her life. Gardner suggests that Cloona became "the most stable and obsessive of her symbols" because of "its connotations of inheritance, entitlement, birthright" ("A'vert to Australianism" 44). While this is a good point, when pondering the significance of this photograph we must also take into consideration the possibility of a desire that is much more fundamental. In his deliberations on the importance of the first shelter Bachelard argues:

> In short, the house we were born in has engraved within us the hierarchy of the various functions of inhabiting. We are the diagram of the functions of inhabiting that particular house, and all the other houses are but variations on a fundamental theme. (15)

What did the first house, which is an "oneiric house, a house of dream-memory," engrave within the young Grimshaw, what hierarchy of inhabiting did it leave (Bachelard 15)? These speculations indicate two possible preoccupations: rootedness and movement. The Grimshaws had occupied the area around Cloona since the late eighteenth century. It was where the family had developed their textile industries, where they had established themselves, and where they were buried. It was also the place Grimshaw had to leave at the age of seven. Cloona's roots, its foundations, its cellars, its dead lying close at hand, could not and did not prevent dispossession. Mobility, as we know, is something Grimshaw sought; it became a way of life for her. Yet, in the letter to Windeyer, written some years after the loss of her parents and also College Gardens, she seems to be experiencing an excess of rootlessness, a mobility that wants a chthonic dimension, even one resting in the shallowest of soils. Perhaps this is what the photograph of Cloona offered Grimshaw—the glimpse of a fragile radicle lying in the Antrim earth. At some level this may have been what life on the *Duchess* provided. During her time on board, Grimshaw experienced a sense of community, a sense of being at home, possibly even a fragile sense of rootedness. For, although foundations are lacking, the *Duchess* does have a cellar: the hold, lying below the surface in a space of chthonic density. Surrounded by the amniotic sea, it is from this uterine enclosure that the boat's roots emanate. One is inclined to think that Grimshaw, an inveterate traveler, would have approved of the anchor as root system. While an indispensable part of the boat, the anchor can be lowered or raised at will; it is a portable root, and, even when it is lowered, standing still means still moving. Caught in the rhythms and pulsations of the sea, an anchored boat is never static. The anchor is a root that is manageable and controllable not controlling; but the subtlety and the freedom that it affords does not lessen the problems that may well ensue if it is lost.

Incorporating subterranean depth, an unconsciousness, the liminal space of the boat, with its hold submerged in the deep, also flings an arm toward the stars. This home has both a cellar and an attic. For Grimshaw the aspirational mast is an imaginative staircase which like Bachelard's house "conquer[ing] its share of the sky […] has the entire sky for its terrace" (53). It is this interstitial perspective, likened to "swinging between heaven and earth" (*In the Strange South Seas* 173), that Grimshaw enjoys up in the cross trees and ratlines. This is an aerial vantage point from which space is distorted: "her little white deck lying below me like a tea-tray covered with walking dolls, her masts at times leaning to leeward until my airy seat was swung far out across the water" (172). Hoisted up in a "boatswain's chair," Annie Brassey, approximately a quarter of a century earlier, likewise relished the view from the masthead: "I was so happy up aloft that I did not care to descend; and it was almost as interesting to obverse what a strange and disproportioned appearance everything and everybody on board the yacht presented from my novel position" (202-3). Both women experience a distortion of space, their base, their terra firma mid-ocean is shrunk to almost unrecognizably small proportions. This is not, however, an anxiety provoking experience. Secure in the knowledge of their umbilical connection to the boat, they seem to find this impression of distance appealing. Indeed, as the masts swing leeward, Grimshaw appears to be moving even further away from the boat, further away from the people who are in it.

There is a sense of liberating isolation here, something which Grimshaw, at various junctures in *In the Strange South Seas*, associates with the ocean:

> All these houses look the one way—across the wide, empty grassy street, between the stems of the leaning palms, to the sunset and the still blue sea. It is a lonely sea, this great empty plain lying below the little town. (184)

Grimshaw is on Niué, and she is happy: "Still I loved Niué, and love it yet" (186), sentiments inspired chiefly by the island's isolation:

> It was so very far away, to begin with. In other islands, with regular steamers, people concerned themselves to some degree about the doings of the outer world, and used to wonder how things were getting on, beyond the still blue bar of sea […] But in Niué, the isolation was complete. (186)

Creating a "long, long trail—long in distance and in time," this "blue bar of sea" offers protection from the outside world (157). But as Grimshaw becomes aware after visiting the "Leper Island" (238) at Penrhyn, it is also a barrier that imprisons. Moved by what she sees as the extreme isolation and melancholia of the place, she writes "Nothing stirs, nothing cries; the earth is silent, the sea empty; and a barrier of thousands of long sea miles […] between us and the world where people live" (242). It is hardly surprising that the sea around such a desolate and depressing place should be viewed as a barrier. Grimshaw expresses similar sentiments when visiting the extremely isolated Malden Island. Malden was a heavily industrialized site where colonial entrepreneurs made vast sums of money from the island's guano reserves. Grimshaw describes Malden as being surrounded by a "prison bar of blue relentless ocean" (225) and "the empty prisoning sea" (225). Incorporating the solidity of the prison bar and the rhythms of the tidal streams, Grimshaw's ocean is a mixture of fixity and fluidity, stasis and flux. However, more often than not, it is the latter. Grimshaw only infrequently conceptualizes the sea as a barrier, something which tends to happen when she is viewing it from the perspective of an island dweller and not from that of a passenger on the schooner. Although at one stage in her journey she opines, "For nine days we ploughed across the same monotonous plain of lonely sea, growing a little duller every day" (216), this lament is far from typical of her travel writing. Unlike Samuel Johnson, who described the boat as a prison "with the chance of being drowned" (qtd. in Boswell 348), the sight of the schooner and the sight of the ocean when viewed from it are, for Grimshaw, in the main, sources of promise. This sensibility may of course be informed by Grimshaw's knowledge that her time on board is limited, and it may also be heightened by the sense of impermanence and, indeed, loss that she associates not only with the *Duchess* but also with South Sea trading vessels in general.

In chapter two of *In the Strange South Seas,* when commenting on the small schooners engaged in the pearling trade around the Paumotus, Grimshaw states:

> I never coveted anything more than I coveted those dainty little vessels. Built in San Francisco, where people know how to build schooners, they were finished like yachts [...] One, a thirty-ton vessel, with the neatest little saloon in the world, fitted with shelves for trading; and a captain's cabin like a miniature liner stateroom, and a toy-like galley [...] was so completely a craft after my own heart that I longed to run away with her, or take her off in my trunk to play with—she seemed quite small enough, though her "beat" covered many thousand miles of sea. (47)

Grimshaw is attracted to the boat because of its size and power. Compact to the last degree, it is a miniature, one which effortlessly consumes sea miles but which, nevertheless, ends up being consumed: "Her bones are bleaching on a coral reef among the perilous pearl atolls, this two years past, and her captain [...] of his bones are coral made" (47). Grimshaw casually remarks that "The pitcher that goes to the well, and the schooner that goes to the pearl islands, are apt to meet with the same fate, in time" (47). The schooner's excellent provenance is not enough to keep it afloat. What chance, then, does the *Duchess* have with her suspect background? Discussing the boat that was her home for four months, Grimshaw tells us that photographing from aloft was only possible when the schooner was steady and "[t]hat was seldom [...] for the *Duchess* had been built in New Zealand, where the good schooners do not come from, and had no more hold of the water than a floating egg" (172). The *Duchess* is not reliable; like all boats (and like Cloona that remained for Grimshaw only as a fragment), it is characterized by impermanence. Grimshaw goes on to add:

> More than one sailing vessel turned out by the same builders had vanished off the face of the ocean, in ways not explained, by reason of the absence of survivors, but dimly guessed at all the same; and I cannot allow that the pirate captain had any just cause of annoyance – even allowing for a master's pride in his ship—when I recommended to him to have the schooner's name painted legibly on her keel before he should leave Auckland on his next northward journey, just "in case." (172)

Grimshaw's dire forecast appears to have been accurate; many years later, reminiscing in an article in the *Blue Book*, she writes:

> In those days I roamed the South Seas in a schooner long since sunk among the corals—the *Countess of Ranfurly*, captained by a little white daredevil who afterward became famous in another quarter of the world as an Antarctic explorer. Any passenger he took had to work passage as well as pay; I learned to go aloft, to "hand, reef and steer," and to use the sixteen-foot oar in the whaleboat. (2)

Grimshaw may simply have made a mistake with regards to the boat's name, but it is more likely that she had changed it, as was her wont, in the travelogue. For there can be little doubt that the above description, complete with reference to learning to steer the vessel (*In the Strange South Seas* 171), managing a sixteen-foot oar (172), and the daredevil captain (174-177), is of Grimshaw's time aboard *Duchess*. Grimshaw was convinced that the schooner would eventually be lost at sea; her forebodings seem to have been correct.

The *Duchess* was a bounded space that was destined to disappear, like the first bounded space that she knew, that anyone knows. As O.V. de Milosz puts it: "I say Mother. And my thoughts are of you, oh, House. / House of the lovely dark summers of my childhood" (qtd. in Bachelard 45). The *schooner* was imbued with the impermanence of the mother/womb/tomb, and of Cloona, the first house; it was a disappearing fragment that could go under at any time. Permeated with the rhythms, pulsations, music, and murmurings of the sea, *Duchess*, like all boats, embodied a strong semiotic dimension. Kristeva associates the semiotic with the "archaic, instinctual, and maternal territory"; and in particular the *chora* (*Desire* 136). Meaning "receptacle" the *chora* is an "economy of primary drives" that is "anterior to any space" (Roudiez 6) as "no space has yet been delineated" (Kristeva, *Desire* 284). As a result "facilitations are localized at a point that absorbs them, and they return like a boomerang to the invoking body, without, however, signifying it as separate" (Kristeva *Desire* 284). And what, if not a reduction in separation (between the subject and the boat), a shrinkage of space to shell-like proportions, is Grimshaw describing when she writes of the schooner that she "coveted more than anything else"(*In the Strange South Seas* 46) and which she presents in miniature? Commenting on miniatures Bachelard states "[t]he cleverer I am at miniaturizing the world, the better I possess it" (150). The habitation of one, and only of one, Grimshaw wants to mark as her own, to possess completely, this boat/home. Like the Barthian boat, Grimshaw's ideal schooner will provide her with "an absolutely finite space"; with its toy-like galley everything is, as Barthes suggests, "at hand" (66); all "facilitations are localized" (Kristeva, *Desire* 284).

Of course separation can only be reduced. The boat can never be anterior to space, nor, indeed, would Grimshaw want it to be. It is possibly true to say that the ultimate assault on our awareness of space is the dive; submersion leads to what Bachelard, as we have seen, refers to as "[o]ne substance, one dimension" (205). For Grimshaw, this complete contact with another substance is not desirable. Grimshaw's sea is both a source of promise and dread, the latter provoked by total immersion. She is not at home in the world of fluvial dusk and shadows; it is the mingling of sea and sky, water and air, a place of brilliant surface color that she desires. As one would expect, the color most often associated with this surface is blue: "the sea is so vividly blue, as we push off in the boat, that I wonder my fingers do not come out sapphire-coloured when I dip them in" (*In the Strange South Seas* 126), "melted turquoise" (137), "shimmering pale blue" (156), "peacock-blue in colour" (199), "blue relentless ocean" (225). Commenting on the development of color perception in young children Kristeva states that "[t]he earliest appear to be those with short wavelengths, and therefore the color blue" (*Desire* 225). Blue is thus connected with the body of the archaic mother and with an absence of any fixed sense of identity. But it is not this alone. For now is a time in the newborn's life when the "I" is in "the process of becoming" (*Desire* 225).[5] Movement away from the maternal body is beginning, and it is a disconnection crucial to survival. The archaic mother is a site both of life and death, a nurturing body that can devour.

Beyond representation, the boundless fluidity of the semiotic is indubitably present in the symbolic as a disruptive destabilizing force. Perhaps the boat illustrates this better than any other space, for the sea's semiotic qualities not only facilitate, but they also confuse, disorientate, and obstruct. If the symbolic/semiotic dialectic ceases because the latter gets the upper hand, as in the case of storms and tempests, the vessel will be consumed. A home in motion, the *Duchess* was a contrapuntal site. Suffused with semiotic qualities—rhythms and pulsations—the schooner is also a bounded patriarchy but one which has a woman, if only for a brief interlude, at its helm. It is a complex space, invoking as it does the womb/tomb/first house, while disrupting any erroneous notion of the pre-social. It is from this bounded space that Grimshaw views the vastness of the Pacific; perhaps it is only from such a clearly demarcated space that such vastness can be contemplated. Jules Supervielle argues that "Too much space smothers us much more than if there were not enough" (qtd. in Bachelard 221). On the *Duchess* Grimshaw's private space is radically circumscribed:

> The cabin had a floor exactly the size of my smallest flat box, which filled it so neatly that I had to stand on the lid all the time I was in my room. It had a bunk about as large as a tight fit in coffins[.] (*In The Strange South Seas* 120)

In his work on the death drive, Freud posits the animate and the inanimate as two distinct states, arguing:

> If we take as a truth that knows no exception that everything living dies for internal reasons—becomes inorganic once again—then we shall be compelled to say that "*the aim of all life is death*" and, looking backwards, that "*inanimate things existed before living ones.*" (Freud, *Beyond* 38)

This longing for an anterior state of absolute inanimation produces extreme anxiety within the organism; the death drive is a mix of desire for and fear of stasis:

> What we are left with is the fact that the organism wishes to die only in its own fashion [...] Hence arises the paradoxical situation that the living organism struggles most energetically against events (dangers, in fact) which might help it to attain its life's aim rapidly—by a kind of short-circuit (Freud, *Beyond* 39)

In her two travel brochures, *Three Wonderful Nations* and *The Islands of the Blest* (dates of publication uncertain), Grimshaw posits tourism as escape from a death-like existence. Travel in the South Sea Islands is a form of rebirth where the tourist who has been:

> starved in adolescence on the diet of the work-a-day world's common exigencies, and buried at last with a counting-house stool for headstone—comes to life again, for a little while under the splendours of a tropic moon. (*The Islands of the Blest* 4)

Beyond the tourist destination, a pale imitation of life is played out in the shadow of the symbolic headstone. In her discussion of death and the aesthetic, Elisabeth Bronfen has observed that "representations of death both articulate an anxiety about and a desire for death, they function like a symptom, which psychoanalytic discourse defines as a repression that fails" (x).

While indicative of anxiety about death, Grimshaw's symptomatic headstone simultaneously attempts to negate it. She depicts death as an event taking place in the world of the Other, an urban world characterized by nullifying routine and batch living, a place that she has left. For the tourist, death can only be held at bay by repeated journeying away from the site of stasis. This provides a clear contrast with Grimshaw's representation of death in *In the Strange South Seas*; here death is not occurring at the life of the Other. The coffin-bed is in Grimshaw's cabin, and the desire for and dread of stasis is not simply tranquillized by the literal *bodying* forth of travel. Rather, the categories animate/inanimate are destabilized. Perhaps they always are, for the death drive may not simply bespeak the fusion of desire/fear but also the realization that, as the biological is subsumed into geological immensity, absolute stasis cannot be guaranteed. The pristine before may always be out of reach. Within the space of the boat, the shell-like cabin and even the coffin-bed are permanently impregnated with motion. Grimshaw's sealed corner is a consuming space, one that enfolds her, holding her still in a sea of movement.

The boat is a space where the polarities stasis/movement, animate/inanimate are challenged. Other modes of transportation can be brought to a definite halt. Once positioned in the element for which it was designed, the boat is always in motion. Even when engines are deadened and the sails and anchors lowered, the boat is never entirely stationary. The *Duchess* provided Grimshaw with a finite space, a space of static movement, a space that was a point of departure and arrival, a home in *the away*, a home that was always in motion. Perhaps shards, maybe even an anchor, may remain on the floor of the vast Pacific, somewhere beyond a space of archaic blue, somewhere beyond representation.

Notes

[1] Grimshaw's first journeys in the Pacific were commissioned by the *Daily Graphic* [London]. The articles which were published in this paper, designed largely to appeal to potential tourists and settlers, later formed the basis of *In the Strange South Seas*. Although this was Grimshaw's second travelogue, it described her first journeys in the Pacific. Susan Gardner suggests that her second travelogue, *From Fiji to the Cannibal Islands* (1907), may have been partly sponsored by established and extremely hard-line settler groups within Fiji.

[2] Quoting Martin S. Day, Susan Gardner briefly mentions that there are differences between land and sea journeys, but she does not explore these in her doctoral dissertation (100).

[3] I am referring here to the open sea. Grimshaw did dive in the pool in Port Moresby during her years in Papua (1907-1934). She described the Port Moresby pool in a letter to Margaret Windeyer as "railed and netted in" (Grimshaw "Autograph"); clearly she felt more confident in this environment than she did in the unfenced ocean.

[4] From its introduction into England, yachting had been associated with colonial capital and the state. Presented to Charles II at the Restoration by the Dutch East India Company, the first yacht in English history was the *Mary*. It was not, however, until the nineteenth century, when England was at the zenith of its imperial power that, yachting truly caught the attention of a sporting elite whose capital was, in many cases, either directly or indirectly, inextricable from colonial adventures.

[5] Kristeva's use of "archaic" corresponds with that of Freud. Freud states that the archaic harks back "to picture-language, to symbolic connections, to conditions, perhaps, which existed before our thought-language had developed" (Freud, "Lecture XIII" 199).

Works Cited

Bachelard, Gaston. *The Poetics of Space*. Trans. Maria Jolas. Boston: Beacon, 1994.

Barthes, Roland. *Mythologies*. Trans. Annette Lavers. London: Jonathan Cape, 1974.

Boswell, James. *Boswell's Life of Johnson*. Ed. George Birbeck Hill. Oxford: Claredon, 1971.

Brassey, Annie. *A Voyage in the Sunbeam*. London: Spottiswoode, 1879.

Bronfen, Elisabeth. *Over Her Dead Body: Death, Femininity and the Aesthetic.* Manchester: Manchester UP, 1996.

Freud, Sigmund. *Beyond The Pleasure Principle. The Standard Edition of the Complete Psychological Works of Sigmund Freud.* Ed. and trans. James Strachey. Vol. 18. London: Hogarth P, 1971.

—. "Lecture XIII: The Archaic Features and Infantilism of Dreams." *The Standard Edition of the Complete Psychological Works of Sigmund Freud.* Ed. and trans. James Strachey. Vol. 15. London: Hogarth P, 1971.

Gardner, Susan. "'A'vert to Australianism': Beatrice Grimshaw and the Bicentenary." *Hecate* 13.2 (1987-88): 31-68.

—. "For Love and Money: Beatrice Grimshaw's Passage to Papua." Diss. Rhodes U, 1985.

Grimshaw, Beatrice. *From Fiji to the Cannibal Islands*. London: Thomas Nelson, 1907.

—. "How I Found Adventure." *Blue Book*. 1939. *Beatrice (Ethel) Grimshaw: A Bibliography in Progress*. Ed. Peter Ruber & Victor A. Berch. 1 Nov. 2003. 17 May 2004. <http://pulprack.com/arch/000107.html>.

—. *In the Strange South Seas*. London: Hutchinson, 1907.

—. *The Islands of the Blest*. Dunedin: The Steam Ship Company of New Zealand, 1910-11 (date of publication uncertain).

—. *Isles of Adventure*. London: Herbert Jenkins, 1930.

—. Letter to Miss Margaret Windeyer. 20 July 1912. State Library of New South Wales, Australia. AG66.

—. *The New New Guinea*. London: Hutchinson, 1910.

—. *Three Wonderful Nations*. Dunedin: The Steam Ship Company of New Zealand, 1910-11 (date of publication uncertain).

—. "Where the Red Gods Call: Beatrice Grimshaw at Home." *The Home, An Australian Quarterly*. Mar. 1921. State Library of New South Wales, Austral. Q059/H: 21, 96.

Kristeva, Julia. *Desire in Language*. Trans. Thomas Gora, Alice Jardine, and Leon S. Roudiez. Oxford: Blackwell, 1980.

—. *Powers of Horror: An Essay on Abjection*. Trans. Leon S. Roudiez. New York: Columbia UP, 1982.

Laracy, Eugenie and Hugh. "Beatrice Grimshaw: Pride and Prejudice in Papua." *Journal of Pacific History* 12 (1987): 54-175.

McClintock, Anne. *Imperial Leather: Race, Gender and Sexuality in the Colonial Contest*. London: Routledge, 1995.

Roudiez, Leon S. Introduction. *Desire in Language*. By Julia Kristeva. Trans. Thomas Gora, Alice Jardine and Leon S. Roudiez. Oxford: Blackwell, 1980.

CHAPTER SEVEN

TRAVEL READING AND TRAVEL WRITING IN LOUISA MAY ALCOTT'S "POPPIES AND WHEAT"

SARAH WADSWORTH

Travel narratives, guide books, literary sightseeing, summer novels, beach and airplane reading, travel journals: from reading in transit to tours of literary landmarks, the connections between literacy and travel are both numerous and perennial in American literature and culture. For Louisa May Alcott, the relationship between literature and travel was a recurring preoccupation that took shape over the course of two trips abroad, numerous domestic journeys, a full-length travel narrative, and a handful of shorter treatments, both fictional and journalistic. Conscious that reading, writing, and traveling are all potentially transformative experiences, Alcott persistently explores the intersection of these pleasurable pursuits in her last published book, a collection of stories titled *A Garland for Girls* (1888). In "Water-Lilies," the fourth story in the sequence, an elderly gentlewoman (and mouthpiece for the author) admonishes a group of young travelers, "Very few girls can read fit to be heard now-a-days" (111). Addressing this deficiency, these late stories of Alcott's offer pointed critiques that directly link reading habits, social class, and formation of character.

Of the seven stories in *Garland*, four directly involve travel, both in the United States and abroad. Of these four, "Poppies and Wheat" offers the most extensive treatment of the intertwined themes of literacy and travel.[1] Drawing on Alcott's first (19 July 1865-19 July 1866) trip to Europe, as companion to a wealthy young woman named Anna Weld, "Poppies and Wheat" can be read as a companion piece to Chapters 8, 16, and 18 of *Little Women, Part Two* (in which Amy travels to Europe as a companion to her aunt and cousin) and to *Shawl-Straps*, a thinly fictionalized account of Alcott's second trip abroad in 1870-71 after the success of *Little Women* had made her internationally renowned as well as financially independent. At the same time, the story provides insight into Alcott's use of her travel narratives, journal entries, and letters from abroad as a source for her fiction and reveals how, by channeling these elements into her didactic fiction, Alcott crafts a distinctive form of travel literature that is both descriptive and prescriptive, teaching by example appropriate ways to conduct one's journey—and one's self—while traveling abroad. Moreover, as a self-contained story that reenacts and comments on a wide array of literacy practices within the context of travel and tourism, "Poppies and Wheat" reveals the intricate and complex ways in which travel *structures* various kinds of narrative (letters, journals, stories, reminiscences) even as narrative itself helps "structure" and make sense of the experience of travel.

An updated version of the fable of the grasshopper and the ant, "Poppies and Wheat" is a study in contrasts in which Alcott pairs a frivolous social butterfly and a dutiful young woman as traveling companions on a grand tour of Europe. Clearly, her own experience attending to the "fretful invalid" (*Journals* 148) Anna Weld informs the story. The departures, however, are ultimately more telling than the parallels. In her journals, Alcott sometimes expressed frustration at Anna's fussiness, her unwillingness to venture outdoors, and the tedium of fetching her cushions and shawls.[2] In "Poppies and Wheat," however, seventeen-year-old Ethel Amory has no such excuses as poor health for her selfish and imperious ways. Indeed, Ethel is "gay" and vibrant, with "sparkling eyes" and a "lively tongue" (147). Yet she is also "a spoiled child [who] usually got her own way" (149). When Ethel is invited to travel abroad with Professor Homer, a family friend who is working on "his great historical work," and his "plain but accomplished and excellent wife" (167), she pleads with her mother to allow her to bring along a French governess for a chaperone.[3] When her mother engages studious Jane Bassett instead, Ethel scarcely bothers to conceal her annoyance.

In contrast, Jane, or Jenny as she is subsequently called, is "a small, quiet person" who dresses simply and has a "sweet, modest face," "intelligent eyes" and "a firm mouth" (148). At twenty (considerably younger than Alcott's thirty three years at the time she first embarked for Europe), Jenny already has had four years of experience as a governess. As the eldest child of a widow, Jenny had to learn "self-reliance and self-control" at an early age, and we are told that hers is a "hard, dutiful life" (150) of instructing young children. While carefree Ethel eagerly anticipates a journey filled with shopping, socializing, and leisure activities, industrious Jenny intends to "improve and enjoy every moment" (149) by learning languages (she already knows three at the outset), studying history, seeing the best works of art, and savoring the company of the Homers and their esteemed friends.[4] At the conclusion of her journey, she hopes her new accomplishments will secure her a teaching position in a girls' school, so that she may leave behind the hard life and low pay of a governess. Thus, Jenny aspires to advance through her own diligence, good character, self-improvement, and (in true Algeresque fashion) good fortune in being able to benefit from the largess of a privileged mentor. Travel, in this scenario, supplies intellectual capital for Jenny, providing her with specific skills and knowledge that have substantial economic value in the teaching market. For Ethel, who resolves not "to poke round over old books and ruins" (156), travel offers a different kind of cultural capital, manifested in enviable social connections, stylish manners, fashionable gowns, and coveted bibelots.

Clearly, in giving us these two opposing characters, Alcott is preparing her readers for a trying journey along a rough and bumpy road. As one might expect, the girls clash, and, when they do, Alcott provocatively frames their conflict in the terms of a class struggle. Nettled by the fact that she has been placed under the supervision of an ordinary American girl nearly her own age, Ethel "makes up her mind to keep Jane Bassett in her place" (151). Observing Ethel's "commanding" attitude, Mrs. Homer admonishes Jenny not to let Ethel "tyrannize" over her and reminds her that she is not to be made a "slave" (152). Instead, insists Mrs. Homer, Jenny must "revolt" so that she can take her "proper place" (153). In evoking the European aristocracy with its downtrodden servant class ("keep Jane Bassett in her place"), the diction in this exchange alerts the reader to the seductiveness of European ways and the danger of yielding to Old World class prejudices and anti-egalitarian codes of behavior. At the same time, in alluding to the recent American past, with its slave revolts and Civil War, Mrs. Homer asserts their ties to their own nation and allies Jenny with its ongoing struggles for justice and freedom. Through the interactions between the two girls, Alcott simultaneously critiques anti-democratic notions of class privilege and lays bare the folly of Americans who seek to emulate the elitism of a class structure rigidly girded by bloodlines and inherited wealth.

Although Alcott's diction here evokes the conflict between a tyrannical ruling class and a disenfranchised underclass, the social categories with which the story is most concerned are defined by culture and learning rather than birth and political or economic power. In his study *Consumerism and American Girls' Literature, 1860-1940*, Peter Stoneley analyzes the ways in which Alcott's fiction (in particular *Little Women* and *An Old Fashioned Girl*) addresses social status in a Gilded Age society characterized in part by shifting definitions of class. As Stoneley convincingly argues, Alcott's fiction exhibits recurring anxieties about conceptions of class that had become increasingly linked to consumerism, consumption, and conspicuous displays of wealth (12). Certainly, "Poppies and Wheat" calls into question the new system of ascribing status on the basis of outward display rather than inward character and accomplishments. To be sure, the text of her story cues readers to recognize at once that responsible Jenny's "proper place" is actually above immature Ethel's.

Ethel is easily dazzled by showy and presumptuous displays of social superiority and needs to be instructed in proper behavior (151), while Jenny's intelligence, good sense, delicacy, and civility unerringly guide her in her relations with others. In introducing Jenny, Alcott couches her description in terms that mingle desirable characteristics of both the servant class and the aristocracy, but the text clearly signals Jenny's gentility: although poor, she is "faithful and discreet" (like a good servant), yet she is also "a true lady in all things" (150). As the journey progresses, literacy provides both a touchstone to gauge and a means to develop the true "nobility" of character that is already abundantly evident in Jane Bassett.

On the voyage out, Ethel is exceedingly taken with a company of girls whom Jenny and Mrs. Homer readily identify as "Daisy Millers." Ethel assiduously cultivates a friendship with these supercilious young women and spends her time aboard ship with them, frolicking, playing cards, sitting on deck late into the night, singing, and telling stories. As a result of unwisely engaging in such wearing and unwholesome activities, Ethel is hit unusually hard by seasickness, as Alcott resorts to strict poetic justice. True to form, good-natured Jenny nurses her through the malaise. During the recuperation, Alcott offers up a priceless cameo of the two girls in which Jenny reposes pensively with a book in her lap, while Ethel lounges beside her on a bearskin, "looking pale and interesting" (158).

Although humbled slightly by her bout of seasickness, Ethel still persists in pursuing a life of frivolity as soon as the party disembarks in the British Isles. She shops for trinkets, buys up extravagant dresses, yearns to mingle with English lords and ladies, and continues to prance around with the Daisy Millers. Meanwhile, Jenny applies herself enthusiastically to the project of self-culture or self-improvement, a task she approaches through a combination of reading, writing, judicious sightseeing, and selective socializing.

In her authoritative study of gender and adolescence in nineteenth-century America, Jane H. Hunter comments on the dominance of a "culture of reading and writing" in Victorian America, in which adolescent girls used reading and writing as "vehicles to self-culture" and character development (39). In "Poppies and Wheat," Alcott outlines several specific applications or uses of literacy that demonstrate how the conventional literary practices girls engaged in at home might be extended and adapted within the context of travel and tourism. First, the narrative suggests that reading is the best preparation for travel. But not just any kind of reading will do: both the content and the approach must be tailored for the occasion. During their ocean crossing, Jenny "reads" and "dreams" about the destinations ahead (156).[5] As he observes her "reading up [her] route," kindly Professor Homer remarks, "Like all young travelers, you cling to your Baedeker" (155). Without a trace of asperity,

Professor Homer criticizes the novice's reliance on the standard guidebook, recognizing that this is a stage she will inevitably pass through with experience before moving on to more substantive fare. And so, indeed, with the learned professor as intellectual guide as well as tour guide, Jenny soon graduates from guide books to history and literature. But "Poppies and Wheat" further suggests that, while *what* one reads is important, *how* one reads is no less crucial. In this passage and elsewhere in "Poppies and Wheat," Alcott emphasizes the vital role of the imagination in the act of reading. Even with her Baedeker, Jenny's reading engages more than mere facts and figures, maps and monetary exchange rates; instead, she "reads" and "dreams" and, in so doing, exercises and enlarges her mind in anticipation of adventures to come. In *The Refinement of America: Persons, Houses, Cities*, a landmark history of gentility in nineteenth-century America, Richard L. Bushman comments on precisely this distinction between storing up information and expanding the mental faculties through productive, active, mindful ways of reading. Citing nineteenth-century authorities on the subject, Bushman explains, "Worldly success in the form of wealth or marriage was a secondary reward; more important, reading carried the diligent student to a higher level of existence" (286):

> While reading supplied the mind with knowledge, one writer believed the aim was to create mind. Some people, he said "overlook the only important office of reading and study, which plainly is the acceleration of our faculties through an increase of mind." And how was mind to grow? "Mind is increased by receiving the mental life of a book, and assimilating it with our own nature, not by hoarding up information in the memory." A stock of knowledge was mere "mechanical" learning. Books properly read "enrich and enlarge the mind, stimulating, inflaming, concentrating its activity." "The greatest genius is he who consumes the most knowledge, and converts it into mind." (287)

In conclusion, Bushman formulates a statement that serves admirably as a gloss on Jenny's aspirations in "Poppies and Wheat": "the mind of the well-read young woman encompassed the universe" (Bushman 287).

The importance of reading in Alcott's text extends beyond its power to contribute to the culturally sanctioned project of self-culture, however. In Scotland, as their journey continues to unfold, Ethel and Jenny have an opportunity to witness how a well-read traveler might improve the journey for others, as well as for herself. As they wend their way through the highlands and lowlands, Mrs. Homer, whose memory is "richly stored with the legends, poetry, and romance which make dull facts memorable and history enchanting" (163), regales her companions with fascinating lore. The sharing of such knowledge is educational for Mrs. Homer's traveling companions, even as it announces her own high level of cultivation. From Mrs. Homer, the girls learn about the sights and scenes around them and about the history, folklore, literature, and culture of Scotland. In addition, Mrs. Homer serves as an exemplary role model for the girls. Her example demonstrates that erudition, far from being unwomanly, can facilitate and even heighten a woman's capacity to nurture, assist, and inspire others—a lesson Alcott was eager to impart.

As Bushman notes, "The cultivated mind had a fund of information that permitted a person to display one's 'parts,' as it was put in the eighteenth century" (286). Certainly, this observation applies to Mrs. Homer, although for her "display" is not the point. Effortlessly, she produces an apt quotation for every famous spot, thoughtfully connecting the scenery and sights to the group's shared literary heritage. Writing of the social function of poetry in "an age of mass memorization" (xliv), Angela Sorby points out that quoting poetry is "a practice of repetition that does not simply repeat but rather forces lines of poetry into new contexts, giving it new use-values" (xlii). Quoting Burns and Scott in the highlands of Scotland is, in a sense, reattaching the poetry to its literal context, a practice that has the dual effect of making the verse more vivid and evocative and making the experience of travel more meaningful and memorable. Lifted from the printed page and integrated into the picturesque scenery before them, the poetry takes on a new dimension in the minds of the listeners, where it will be assimilated into their immediate response to the experience, incorporated into their subsequent memories of it, and perhaps later passed on to others through future recitations. Jenny, who admires Mrs. Homer tremendously, embraces this process of assimilation and transmittal as she resolves to "learn some of the fine bits" in Mrs. Homer's copy of Burns and "make them [her] own" so that she "may be to some-one by-and-by what dear Mrs. Homer is to [her and Ethel]" (165).[6]

The Scottish episode offers a decisive reflection on social class as well, as Jenny relates in a letter to her mother and sisters how, on a tour of Holyrood, Mrs. Homer charms an elderly gentleman with her fine quotations.[7] When the gentleman turns out to be Lord Cumberland, Alcott makes the point that good breeding gives rise to good taste, even as the story illustrates that true "nobility" is achieved through cultivation. Here, the mastery of British poetry and the social competence to use that mastery effectively establish a common ground between two people of "noble" character from opposite sides of the Atlantic: the titled English gentleman and the refined American lady. When the courtly Lord Cumberland graciously pronounces Mrs. Homer "'a book of elegant extracts'" (166), he alludes to a particular type of anthology, known in the nineteenth-century as a "memory gem" (Hunter 72), specifically conceived to promote self-cultivation and character-building through memorization of the "best" literature. By emphasizing the shared literary heritage of Mrs. Homer and Lord Cumberland, the story makes a larger point about the culture these two share: a culture of refinement that has developed along different paths in the two countries only to converge as the *best* both countries have to offer. Gentility, the story suggests, may be *bred* in the upper classes of Great Britain, but in America it is *cultivated* in intelligent individuals of noble character and lofty ideals.

Of course, Jenny, a girl of rich inner resources and sterling character, does not need to rely on others for her literary reference points. Further developing the notion that reading should exercise the imagination as well as the memory, Alcott allows us to observe Jenny as she tours Scotland with many remembered texts in mind, thus illustrating how the experience of travel is enhanced when one views landscapes, landmarks, and other notable scenes through the lens of great literature.[8] While Ethel's reading is confined to undistinguished novels and illustrated newspapers replete with royal events, Jenny arrives in Scotland with an imagination already vivified by her past reading of classic texts. With an implicit critique of contemporary reading tastes, Alcott explains that Jenny "had not scorned Scott's novels as old-fashioned" (164). Consequently, as she explores Scotland she is able to "people the cottages and castles with his heroes and heroines," "croon Burns's sweet songs to herself as she visit[s] his haunts," and go "about in a happy sort of dream, with her head full of Highland Mary, Tam o' Shanter, field-mice and daisies or [fight] terrific battles with Fitz-James and Marmion, and [try] if 'the light harebell' would 'raise its head from her airy tread,' as it did from the Lady of the Lake's famous foot" (164). Although Ethel scoffs at this dreamy mode of sightseeing, Jenny revels in it, and "so," Alcott effuses, "she absorbed Scotch poetry and romance with the mist and the keen air from the moors, and bloomed like the bonnie heather she loved to wear" (164). Through this almost visceral integration of literature, imagination, geography, physical sustenance, and personal adornment, Alcott reveals how the act of reading can invest lived experience with an imaginative, almost spiritualized, dimension that is at once invigorating, ennobling, and beautiful.

Reading and travel continue to coalesce in "Poppies and Wheat" as the characters embark on a course of literary sightseeing. In London, Jenny visits the British museum, where she attends to Professor Homer, and dines at "a famous chophouse where Johnson had drunk oceans of tea" (173). At Westminster Abbey, she sits "spellbound" in Poets' Corner while Mrs. Homer "name[s] the illustrious dead around them" (169). And, while Ethel ogles wax-work celebrities at Madame Tussaud's and strains to catch sight of flesh-and-blood royals in London's fashionable spots, Jenny has the rare privilege of seeing Browning, hearing Irving, having tea with Jean Ingelow, and meeting the distinguished politician William Gladstone (172).

Significantly, Jenny's glimpses of illustrious figures and notable sites correspond—but imperfectly—with Alcott's own experience during her first trip abroad as companion to Anna Weld. While staying with Peter Alfred Taylor and his wife in their house in Notting Hill, Alcott saw "many interesting persons," including Jean Ingelow and, on a visit to the House of Commons, Gladstone (*Journals* 151). In addition, in *Shawl-Straps* Alcott describes a visit to the home of "a Radical M. P." whose guests included Jean Ingelow (206) and "lunch at Dolly's (the dark, little chop-house, which Johnson, Goldsmith, and the other worthies used to frequent in the good old times)" (204-05). Jenny's lack of enthusiasm for royal-watching also mirrors Alcott's own experience. In a letter to a friend, written from Nice, Alcott related that her old landlady, who had once been governess to Queen Victoria's daughters, offered to furnish her with letters of introduction addressed to her friends at Court. Commenting on the possibility of "get[ting] peeps at Royalty," Alcott confessed that she had no particular wish to see them and admitted, "I'd rather see Dickens, Browning & Carlyle than her Majesty & the nine royal children in a row" (*Selected Letters* 112). During her subsequent stay in London, Moses Coit Tyler, an American friend, gratified this preference by taking her on a literary tour of London, highlighting particularly those sites associated with Dickens and his novels. Tyler, who went on to become professor of rhetoric and literature at the University of Michigan and may have been a model for Professor Homer, reported in a letter to his wife that Alcott was "a jolly Yankee girl, full of the old Nick and thoroughly posted on English literature, so that it is great fun to take her about, as she appreciates all the literary associations" (*Selected Letters* 115). Although Alcott was evidently quite disappointed in Dickens's "foppishness" (*Selected Letters* 115) at a reading she attended at St. James's Hall, she clearly reveled in the side of London Coit showed her, with its "memorable mixture of shrines & shillings, history & happiness, mud & metaphysics" (*Selected Letters* 115). She even wrote up a slightly fictionalized version of the day's adventures, publishing it in the *Independent* as "A Dickens Day" (26 December 1867), and included a version of their "Dickens Pilgrimage" in *Shawl-Straps* (218).

Like Alcott, most middle-class Americans became acquainted with England first through the fiction they grew up with. The rise of realism during the later nineteenth century further contributed to the blurring of boundaries between the realistic but imaginatively recreated worlds of fiction and the real but faraway and oft-imagined worlds in which this fiction was set. Sightseeing excursions such as the one Alcott described in "A Dickens Day" involve a self-conscious erasing of the border between fiction and real life as the real-life traveler inserts herself into the physical space memorably evoked and preserved in the literary text. One nineteenth-century correspondent wrote to a traveling friend with precisely this kind of imaginative border-crossing in mind:

> You are now probably fairly domesticated in Old London. I like to think of you as gradually making the acquaintance not only of Parliament House & Westminster Hall & Abbey, of Hyde Park & St. James, of St Pauls & the Tower

> the Strand & the Bridges—but also those out of the way places which are to us almost as classic as the others thro' the works of Dickens & Thackeray. Undoubtedly whether you seek them or not you will sometimes be near the Coal Hale [?] & Bevis Marks, the dilapidated houses & wharfs that witnessed (as we imagine) the trials & wanderings of David Copperfield & Sitterwell, the adventures of Sam Weller & Mr. Pickwick; the fleet & Old Bailey, and all the wonders of the Great Metropolis.[9]

As this fanciful letter suggests, fictional characters seemingly become more "real" to the reader who visits their haunts and habitations and, potentially, even more real than "actual events and people" (see *Shawl-Straps* 220). In addition, real locations (even otherwise obscure ones) might acquire a personal significance in the mind of the traveler through the textual connection between physical geography and fictional setting. In *Shawl-Straps*, after visiting sites associated with "Pendennis and Fanny, John Westlock and little Ruth Pinch," Alcott records, "For their sakes, Livy [Lavinia] went to see the place; and for their sakes she still remembers that green spot in the heart of London, with the June sunshine falling on it as it fell that day" (220). Writing in her journal of her first trip to London, Alcott recorded how she occupied her time while the "Weld encumbrances" (Anna and her brother George) were otherwise engaged ("Anna [. . .] ill & Geo. sight-seeing"):

> I amused myself in my usual quiet way looking well about me & writing down all I saw in my pocket diary and letters. Went to Parks, Westminster Abbey & some of the famous streets. Felt as if I'd got into a novel while going about in the places I'd read so much of. Saw no one I knew & thought English weather abominable. (*Journals* 141)

Nevertheless, although Alcott gleefully visited sites associated with cherished novels, she evidently deemed this particular type of literary sightseeing more suitable for the more mature audiences of the *Independent* and *Shawl-Straps* than for the more impressionable juvenile readers of *A Garland for Girls*. Jenny's literary sightseeing is confined to face-to-face meetings with authors and visits to sites associated with authors' *lives*—not their fictional creations.

Alcott's journal entries highlight a kind of reciprocity or symbiosis among various kinds of literacy practices. As Hunter notes, "Girls read and wrote in tandem, often patterning their writing on their reading, and also relying on their reading experiences as the stuff of their diary writing" (Hunter 57). As in Alcott's own experience, in "Poppies and Wheat" letter- and journal- writing provide a crucial means of preserving impressions and memories of travel and sharing experiences with those at home. According to Hunter, diary-writing, for Victorian girls, also served to moderate emotions, encourage restraint, and promote commitment to one's duties within the family. It is this latter function—promoting duty—that Alcott particularly stresses in "Poppies and Wheat." Tiring of the "'whirl and gayety'" of London, Mrs. Homer and Jenny "[plan] more quiet excursions with some hours each day for rest and the writing and reading which all wise tourists make a part of their duty and pleasure" (167-68). Analyzing girls' diary-keeping in nineteenth-century America, Hunter remarks: "Within vessels chartered and christened by parents, Victorian girls embarked on imaginative journeys which did not threaten to take them too far from home" (Hunter 51). Although most girls did write from their homes, travel offers a special impetus to the diarist, providing abundant material to write about as well as a built-in narrative structure patterned after the traveler's itinerary. Etymologically, "journey" and "journal" are related, sharing the common Latin root *diēs* ("day"), a connection that is highlighted in Jenny's daily practice of writing about her day's travels in a journal that she will eventually share with her family at home. As she gains experience and becomes increasingly adept at sifting her impressions and committing her thoughts to paper, Jenny adds "new and famous names [. . .] to the list in her journal," and before long "the artless pages were rich in anecdotes, descriptions, and comments on the day's adventures" (170). Mrs. Homer also writes dutiful "journal-letters" (a hybrid form specially adapted to offset the expense and vagaries of international postage) to "the anxious mothers at home" (158); and Jenny supplements her writing with sketches for her portfolio. As Brian Dolan remarks of early women travelers, "travel writing became an end itself and the achievement of traveling" (278), an observation that applies to Jenny as well as to the eighteenth-century British women Dolan considers.

Just as Alcott kept in close contact with her family at home through the exchange of letters, Jenny, too, remains connected to her mother, even while abroad, through their correspondence. But letter-writing serves an additional purpose in "Poppies and Wheat." Private writing, in the form of both letters and diary-keeping, allows Jenny to hone her writing and fulfill her daughterly duty, while helping her to extend her skills. As a result, when the opportunity arises, Jenny is fully prepared to step up to new responsibilities. One day, when Mrs. Homer is incapacitated by a nervous headache, Jenny is able to assist Professor Homer by writing up his research notes (170). In so doing, she further proves her intellectual mettle, along with her commitment to duty and her worthiness of the Homers' mentorship.

During this phase of their journey, Alcott has further occasion to shine a light on her travelers' ambivalent responses to Old World class systems. Ethel continues to be fascinated by royalty, but she is not the only one to fall under their spell. Following their lunch at the chophouse, Jenny and Professor Homer stroll in the park, where they have the good fortune to meet the Duchess of

S______ and her companion, who invite them to ride along in their carriage, attended by "a white-wigged coachman perched aloft and two powdered footmen erect behind" (173). Upon returning to their hotel, Professor Homer "observe[s] the new air of dignity which Jane unconsciously assumed as an obsequious waiter flew before to open the door" (174). When Jenny good-naturedly admits that she does "like splendor" and *was* "rather set up" to think she had "spoken to a live duchess" (although, in good democratic fashion, she particularly admires the Duchess's "charming manners," simplicity of dress, and pleasant conversation, "as if she didn't feel a bit above us" [174]), Professor Homer graciously instructs her as to the true meaning of nobility:

> "That is just it, my dear; she *is* a noble woman in every sense of the word, and has a right to her title. Her ancestors were king-makers, and she is Lady-in-waiting to the Queen; yet she leads the charities of London, and is the friend of all who help the world along. I'm glad you have met her, and seen so good a sample of a true aristocrat. We Americans affect to scorn titles, but too many of us hanker for them in secret, and bow before very poor imitations of the real thing. Don't fill your journal with fine names, as some much wiser folk do, but set down only the best, and remember, 'All that glitters is not gold.'" (175)

Once again, Alcott is alerting her readers to spurious and superficial social distinctions, but at the same time she (through Professor Homer, a reliable guide) is also ascribing merit to the "real thing," genuine nobility. The story thus encourages readers to discriminate on the basis of refinement of character rather than wealth and privilege, without repudiating inherited class entitlements altogether. Yet here, too, the contradiction is consistent with Alcott's emphasis on genteel conduct. Bushman's study, *The Refinement of America*, helps resolve the ambiguity by linking the expansion of gentility in nineteenth-century America to the nation's continuing fascination with all things royal:

> At a time when the Revolution had ended the principles of monarchy and aristocracy and the forces of capitalist enterprise were leading Americans into industrialization, Americans modeled their lives after the aristocrats of a society that was supposedly repudiated at the founding of the nation. The spread of gentility speaks for the enduring allure of royal palaces and great country estates, for the enticing mystery of nobility and gentry, for the enchantment of those seemingly exalted lives, for enthrallment with their grace of movement, speech, and costume. The hold of the old regime on the imaginations of Americans cannot be overlooked in explaining the spread of refinement and the creation of a mass market. (xix)

"Poppies and Wheat" is a prime illustration of these paradoxical attitudes toward social class. While maintaining that the girls are responsible for holding themselves to the highest standards of behavior, the story also suggests that, on some level, birth and breeding do matter. Like many of her contemporaries, Alcott seems to scorn Americans who pant after royalty, yet (as in the case of Lord Cumberland and the Duchess of S______) she is only too willing to trot out nobles (refined, never showy) to substantiate or authenticate her own bid for good taste and breeding.

In many respects, "Poppies and Wheat" charts its protagonists' personal growth and transformation as they embark on a literal journey from America through Europe and pursue a metaphorical journey from their respective stages of adolescence to full, or, in Ethel's case, partial maturity.[10] Reading, writing, and travel serve important functions in Jenny's rites of passage, as she develops into a patient, cultured, restrained individual true to the high ideals of democratic citizenship and genteel domesticity. As the story progresses, these functions become embodied and symbolized in the literary souvenirs Jenny acquires. Susan Stewart offers insight into the manner in which souvenirs relate to the individual's life-journey and, in particular, to points of personal transformation: "The souvenir [. . .] is intimately mapped against the life history of an individual; it tends to be found in connection with rites of passage (birth, initiation, marriage, and death) as the material sign of an abstract referent: transformation of status" (139). In Germany, while Ethel is buying up so many "brittle" trinkets that she needs to purchase a new trunk to hold them all, Jenny "content[s] herself with a German book, Kaulbach's Goethe Gallery, and a set of ornaments for each sister" (177).[11] Clearly, these souvenirs function as material signs that refer to a particular rite of passage—the Grand Tour. Yet Alcott reserves a special souvenir—one that holds value quite apart from its material form—to refer to the most meaningful transformations Jane experiences. In Geneva, for Jenny's twenty-first birthday, Mrs. Homer presents her with a set of little volumes like the Burns she had admired earlier. Pleased by the gifts she has received, Jenny spends "a very happy day [. . .] quietly [. . .] sitting by the lake enjoying the well-chosen extracts from Shakespeare, Wordsworth, Byron, Burns, Scott, and other descriptive poets, and writing loving letters home" (180). Just as in Scotland Jenny experienced the landscape and landmarks through the lens of literature, so on the Continent she learns to experience literature through the lens of travel. From this point forward, armed with "her valuable little library, her industrious pencil, and her accomplished guides," Jenny derives even greater satisfaction from her travels, as the fine literature she reads illuminates her route from site to site around the shores of Lake Geneva. Alcott elaborates:

> Calvin and Geneva, Voltaire and Ferney, De Staël and Coppet, Gibbon's garden at Lausanne, Byron's Prisoner at Chillon, Rousseau's chestnut grove at Clarens, and all the legends, relics, and memories of Switzerland's heroes, romancers,

> poets, and philosophers were carefully studied, recorded, and enjoyed; and when at last they steamed away toward Paris, Jenny felt as if her head and her heart and one little trunk held richer treasures than all the jewelry in Geneva. (180)

In this way, reading and traveling crystallize to create Jenny's most precious "souvenirs": her journal, her sketchbook, her guides, and the treasured volumes of verse. Theorizing about the narrative function of scrapbooks, photo albums, baby books, and similar compendia, Stewart reflects, "It is significant that such souvenirs often appropriate certain aspects of the book in general; we might note especially the way in which an exterior of little material value envelops a great 'interior significance,' and the way both souvenir and book transcend their particular contexts" (139). The book *as* souvenir is, I would argue, a special case in which the "exterior of little material value envelops" an interior that is doubly significant. The book itself transcends the context of the material object (that is, the *text* transcends the physical materials on/in/with which it is inscribed), while the book as souvenir achieves an additional degree of transcendence (and significance) through its function as memento. In "Poppies and Wheat," however, Jenny's literary souvenirs—books enveloping this double "interior significance"—do not so much transcend their immediate contexts as they *transform* those contexts into transcendent realms—eternal, luminous, and permeated with significance in the mind of the enlightened reader-traveler.

According to Professor Homer, "a well-stored mind [is] a tool-chest with which one could carve one's way" (182). As a teacher, Jenny knows that her "tools are knowledge, memory, taste, the power of imparting what [she] know[s], good manners, sense, and—patience" (182). This last attribute has truly been honed on the journey, since as Ethel's companion her patience has been sorely tried. But in the end, Alcott shows that Jenny is not the only one who has grown and that Ethel has benefited from Jenny's company as well. In fact, Jenny has amply proven herself as an educator by imparting some valuable lessons to Ethel. In keeping with the overarching thematic device of *A Garland for Girls*, which rests on an intricate and sustained use of flower symbolism, Alcott conveys this lesson through floral imagery. While driving from the ruins of Hohenstein one afternoon, the girls pause to pick flowers with which to decorate their hats. Ethel gathers "a great bouquet of scarlet poppies," while Jenny collects "a handful of green wheat" (177). When Ethel finds fault with Jenny's homely bouquet, Jenny retorts, "'I like my honest breadmaking wheat better than your opium flowers" (178), and, of course, this implicit contrast between wholesome nourishment and gaudy delusion reflects the characters of the two girls. When Professor Homer notices her bouquet of wheat, he observes that Jenny "look[s] as if [she] had been gleaning" (177), and this "gleaning," like the journey itself, becomes both literal and metaphoric. Stewart's comments on the symbolic nature of souvenirs are illuminating in this context. "Because of its connection to biography and its place in constituting the notion of the individual life," Stewart explains, "the memento becomes emblematic of the worth of that life and of the self's capacity to generate worthiness" (139).

Given this link between souvenirs, symbolism, and perceptions of self-worth, it is not surprising that the task of repacking their trunks at the conclusion of their journey should afford an opportunity for personal reflection and self-evaluation. Indeed, packing up at journey's end constitutes something of a ritual, in fiction as in life, as the traveler takes stock of her possessions, receptive to the memories of people and places visited that the various articles recall. Limitations of space heighten the need to appraise their intrinsic and sentimental value in order to decide which to retain and which to jettison. In "Poppies and Wheat" Alcott prepares the girls for this inevitable reckoning by allowing Ethel to contemplate the industrious life to which Jenny expects to return. Having been treated with kindness and forbearance by "dear Jenny," Ethel is now able to feel pity and admiration for her chaperone, as well as regret and remorse for her own conduct and lack of gratitude. Following her examination of conscience, Ethel repents and resolves to make it up to Jenny by giving her a "holiday" during their final days in Paris. Once again, however, poetic justice swiftly intervenes as Ethel falls ill from over-indulging in pastry and is consequently "laid up" with "a sharp bilious attack." In a passage that surely derives from her own experiences with Anna Weld, even as it mirrors the story's earlier scene of seasickness, Alcott shows how Ethel is brought low by illness while Jenny further rises in her esteem by nursing her back to health.

Directly following this reversal, the packing-up scene finds Ethel unusually pensive and self-critical and, at long last, prepared to give Jenny her due. In this frame of mind, her souvenirs seem to her so much "rubbish," and as she ruminates over them "the penitent" becomes "conscious of a strong desire to [thank] Jane Bassett [. . .] for all her patient and faithful care." To Jenny, she makes a series of resolutions—"to be better prepared" and "really study" and "not be a fool." Determined to make amends, she proposes that Jane return home with her and become her governess for the winter, tutoring her in the foreign languages she has failed to master. But Ethel's offer of "atonement" is promptly overshadowed by an even better reward for Jane. A letter from home reveals that the Homers have written to her mother to invite Jenny to accompany them to Rome for the winter and to Greece in the spring. Jenny is overjoyed at her good fortune (not seeing Rome had been her one regret), and Ethel, who has finally become "her best self," is happy for her deserving friend.

At the conclusion of the story, a humbler and wiser (i.e., more worthy) Ethel compares her hat, decorated with "the faded artificial flowers" that have replaced the fragile, ephemeral poppies, and Jenny's hat, with its sturdy yet still attractive spray of dried wheat. With a note of contrition, she concedes: "You were right, Jenny. My poppies are worthless, and my harvest a very poor one. Your wheat fell in good ground, and you will glean a whole stack before you go home" (192). The "good ground" consists of Jenny's nurturing character and fertile mind, which has been carefully prepared, enriched, and cultivated through reading, writing, and travel. Throughout "Poppies and Wheat," Alcott offers glimpses of crass social climbers who flaunt their outward wealth, alongside inconspicuous nobles who are recognizable (by the equally refined) through their impeccable manners and rewarding conversation. Ethel's relenting at the end of the story shows that she has abandoned her haughty, superior ways and learned to discriminate between these two classes, that is, between genuine "gold" and mere "glitter." Having learned this lesson, she concedes to Jenny her rightful position as one whose unmistakable nobility of character richly merits both recognition and respect.

Near the beginning of "Poppies and Wheat," we are told that Ethel is "wild with delight at the idea" of joining the Homers on their journey for "it was a rare opportunity to travel in such company" (148-89). Alcott's travel fiction is itself "a rare opportunity to travel in such company" and to benefit, like Ethel and Jenny, from the "society of better companions." In the same story, she introduces readers to characters she refers to as "our fellow-travellers" (147), including Jane Bassett, who is to be our "bosom friend." In using these first-person plural possessives, Alcott unites author, readers, and fictional characters, implicitly imagining her readers as travelers and inviting us to participate in a voyage of discovery. As these tropes suggest, reading is itself a journey and the journey a text to be created, inscribed, and interpreted. In "Poppies and Wheat," Alcott explores the unique synergy between literacy and travel in nineteenth-century America, as her characters absorb literature through their travels while simultaneously enriching their travels through the medium of literature. Through the contrasting experiences of Ethel Amory and Jane Bassett, "Poppies and Wheat" suggests that travel can effect a kind of consummation between reader and text, wedding the narrative of lived experience to the narrative of text and thereby elevating both to a higher plain of existence. As Alcott exhorts at the end of *Shawl-Straps*:

> Dear Amandas, Matildas, and Lavinias, why delay? Wait for no man, but take your little store and invest it in something far better than Paris finery, Geneva jewelry, or Roman relics. Bring home empty trunks, if you will, but heads full of new and larger ideas, hearts richer in the sympathy that makes the whole world kin, hands readier to help on the great work God gives humanity, and souls elevated by the wonders of art and the diviner miracles of Nature.
>
> Leave *ennui* and discontent, frivolity and feebleness, among the ruins of the old world, and bring home to the new the grace, the culture, and the health which

will make American women what now they just fail of being, the bravest, brightest, happiest, and handsomest women in the world. (225-26)

Notes

[1] The other stories that involve travel are “Pansies,” “Water-Lilies,” and “Mountain-Laurel and Maidenhair.”

[2] In her journal, Alcott wrote, “I tried my best to suit & serve her but don’t think I did so very well, yet many would have done still worse I fancy, for hers is a very hard case to manage & needs the patience & wisdom of an angel” (*Journals* 142). Six months later, she reflected, “I’m rather fond of her but she wears upon me & we are best apart” (*Journals* 150). Rereading these entries twenty years later, a greatly debilitated Alcott was able to sympathize with Anna, inserting into her journal the comment: “Now, having been a nervous invalid myself, I understand what seemed whims, selfishness & folly at the time I was with A.” (*Journals* 148).

[3] The relationship between the Homers is similar to that between a prominent man of science and his “helpmeet” wife in “Pansies,” another story in *A Garland for Girls* that explores the intersections of gender and reading in nineteenth-century America. See Wadsworth, “A Blue and Gold Mystique.”

[4] Jenny’s facility with languages contrasts markedly with Alcott’s difficulties learning French (she complained in her journal how she “grubbed away at French with no master & small success” [*Journals* 142]) and with Jo March’s aversion to studying French, which costs her a trip to Europe. See also *Selected Letters* 150.

[5] Of her own transatlantic crossing in July 1865, Alcott recorded in her diary, “No pleasant people on board so I read & whiled away the long days as I best could” (*Journals* 141).

[6] Sarah Robbins’s recent study of maternal literacy narratives is relevant to the way in which Alcott constructs a gendered, generational (i.e., “maternal”) line of literary influence that extends from the matronly Mrs. Homer to her young, female charges. See *Managing Literacy, Mothering America*.

[7] As William Merrill Decker explains, “The letter is ever a locus of class markers: masteries of protocol, refinements of taste, levels of cultivation, grades of literacy” (14).

[8] Scotland was a particularly popular site for Americans to pursue literary pilgrimages. Stowe’s journey through Scotland in *Sunny Memories of Foreign Lands* is laced with allusions to Scott, and in *Glimpses of Three Coasts* Helen Hunt Jackson devotes an entire chapter to “A Burns Pilgrimage.”

[9] J. C. Parsens, letter to Alfred P. Rockwell. 22 October 1857.

[10] As Brian Dolan remarks, “It is no accident that the metaphor of travel has long been used to represent the twists and turns, discoveries and drudgery of intellectual and psychological development” (5).

[11] Wilhelm von Kaulbach (1805-74) was a German Romantic painter, illustrator, and muralist. *The Goethe Gallery*, published by James R. Osgood, was a quarto volume containing twenty-one full-page heliotype engravings from Kaulbach’s original drawings, accompanied by explanatory text. Possibly, Alcott had *The Goethe Gallery* in mind when she wrote in her journal, “To Cologne on the 9th & the country we passed through was like a big picture book” (*Journals* 142). The reference to Goethe may also

allude to what she clearly regarded as the Weld's philistinism. A marginal notation, inserted at a later date into her travel journal, records: "The W[eld]s said, 'Who was Goethe to fuss about?'" (*Journals* 147).

Works Cited

Alcott, Louisa May. *Aunt Jo's Scrap-Bag*. Vol. 2. *Shawl-Straps*. Boston: Roberts Brothers, 1872.

—. *A Garland for Girls*, 1888 [c. 1887]. New York: Grosset & Dunlap, 1908.

—. *The Journals of Louisa May Alcott*. Ed. Joel Myerson and Daniel Shealy. Assoc. Ed. Madeleine B. Stern. Athens, GA: U of Georgia P, 1997.

—. *The Selected Letters of Louisa May Alcott*. Ed. Joel Myerson and Daniel Shealy. Assoc. Ed. Madeleine B. Stern. Athens, GA: U of Georgia P, 1995.

Bushman, Richard L. *The Refinement of America: Persons, Houses, Cities*. New York: Knopf, 1992.

Decker, William Merrill. *Epistolary Practices: Letter Writing in America before Telecommunications*. Chapel Hill: U of North Carolina P, 1998.

Dolan, Brian. *Ladies of the Grand Tour: British Women in Pursuit of Enlightenment and Adventure in Eighteenth-Century Europe*. New York: Harper Collins, 2001.

Hunter, Jane H. *How Young Ladies Became Girls: The Victorian Origins of American Girlhood*. New Haven: Yale UP, 2002.

Jackson, Helen Hunt. "A Burns Pilgrimage." *Glimpses of Three Coasts*. Boston: Roberts Brothers, 1886.

Parsens, J. C. Letter to Alfred P. Rockwell. 22 October 1857. *The Nation* Papers bMS Am 1083.2(65). Houghton Library, Harvard University.

Robbins, Sarah. *Managing Literacy, Mothering America: Women's Narratives on Reading and Writing in the Nineteenth Century*. Pittsburgh: U of Pittsburgh P, 2004.

Sorby, Angela. *Schoolroom Poets: Childhood, Performance, and the Place of American Poetry, 1865-1917*. Hanover, NH: University Press of New England, 2005.

Stewart, Susan. *On Longing: Narratives of the Miniature, the Gigantic, the Souvenir, the Collection*. Durham, NC: Duke UP, 1993.

Stoneley, Peter. *Consumerism and American Girls' Literature, 1860-1940*. Cambridge: Cambridge UP, 2003.

Stowe, Harriett Beacher. *Sunny Memories of Foreign Lands*. 1884. New York: Cosimo Classics, 2005.

Wadsworth, Sarah A. "A Blue and Gold Mystique: Reading the Material Text in Louisa May Alcott's 'Pansies' and Ticknor & Fields's *Blue and Gold Series*." *Harvard Library Bulletin* 11.2 (Summer 2000): 55–80.

CONTRIBUTORS

Jeanne Dubino is Professor of English and Chair at Appalachian State University in North Carolina. She has taught in colleges and universities in New England, Turkey, Kenya, and most recently Louisiana. Her most recent publications include articles on Mary Wortley Montagu's *Turkish Embassy Letters*, nineteenth-century British women travelers to Turkey, Kenyan fiction, and Virginia Woolf's essays. Currently she is working on a larger project on British representations of Kenya.

Shoshannah Ganz earned her Ph.D. in Canadian Literature at the University of Ottawa in 2006, with a dissertation entitled *Canadian Literary Pilgrimage: From Colony to Post-Nation.* She has delivered papers and published on a number of Canadian authors, including Robertson Davies, Margaret Atwood, Richard B. Wright, Timothy Findley, Oliver Goldsmith, Miriam Waddington, and Rachel Korn. She writes regularly for *The Journal of Canadian Poetry* and is currently co-editing a collection of essays on Canadian poet Al Purdy as part of the Reappraisals series due to come out with University of Ottawa Press in 2007.

Marguerite Helmers is Professor of English at the University of Wisconsin Oshkosh. She is the author of *The Elements of Visual Analysis* (2006) and *Writing Students* (1995), editor of *Intertexts: Reading Pedagogy in College Writing Classrooms* (2002), and co-editor with Charles Hill of *Defining Visual Rhetorics* (2004). She has contributed articles to the scholarly journals *College English*, the *Journal of Advanced Composition*, and the electronic journals *Enculturation* and *Kairos*.

Tilar Mazzeo is Assistant Professor of English in the Department of English at Colby College, where she specializes in travel writing and Romantic-period literature and culture. She is the editor of several volumes of late eighteenth- and early nineteenth-century British travel writing, including voyages describing colonial relations with the Middle East, India, and the Americas. She is the author of *Plagiarism and Literary Property in the Romantic Period* (2006).

Clare McCotter is a member of the Department of Languages and Literature at the University of Ulster. Her publications include articles on Beatrice Grimshaw in the *Journal of Tourism and Cultural Change* (2006), the *Irish Feminist Review* (2006), and *Hecate* (2006).

Russ Pottle is Academic Dean and senior Professor of Literature at Saint Joseph Seminary College, in Saint Benedict, Louisiana. He has published work on travel writing and the early narratives of Herman Melville, and he has contributed to a variety of college-level composition textbooks.

Valerie Smith is Associate Professor of English at Quinnipiac University in Hamden, Connecticut. She holds a Ph.D. from the University of Connecticut.

Sarah Wadsworth is assistant professor of English at Marquette University. She is the author of *In the Company of Books: Literature and Its "Classes" in Nineteenth-Century America* (2006). At present she is completing a book-length study of the women's library of the World's Columbian Exposition in collaboration with Wayne A. Wiegand.

SUBJECT INDEX

AUTHOR INDEX

Note: Page numbers in italic indicate bibliographic entries.